BLOOD MONEY

BLOOD MONEY
The CIVIL WAR *and the* FEDERAL RESERVE

JOHN REMINGTON GRAHAM
FOREWORD BY DAVID AIKEN

Pelican Publishing Company
GRETNA 2006

Library of Congress Cataloging-in-Publication Data

Graham, John Remington, 1940-
  Blood money : the Civil War and the Federal Reserve / by John
Remington Graham ; foreword by David Aiken.
    p. cm.
  ISBN-13: 978-1-58980-398-5 (pbk. : alk. paper)
  1. Money—United States—History—19th century. 2. Monetary pol-
icy—United States—History—19th century. 3. Federal Reserve
banks—History—19th century. 4. United States—History—Civil
War, 1861-1865. I. Title.
  HG525.G665 2006
  973.7'11—dc22
                                                          2006007762

Published by Pelican Publishing Company, Inc.
1000 Burmaster Street, Gretna, Louisiana 70053

"Rather than assume the care of the slaves, they would control labor with the use of capital. It necessarily followed that, when the laborer ceased to be of service because of sickness or old age, he would be of no concern to capital. He could either get well or die without the capitalists being obliged to provide medical attention or bury the dead. Such was the interest that capital had in the result of the Civil War. The people of this country poured out both their treasure and their blood to establish the political and industrial independence of humanity, and the mercenary capitalists turned a trick of finance and converted the enormous sacrifice made by the people during that struggle into a victory for capital in order that they might enforce upon humanity the industrial slavery that the trusts preferred rather than the chattel slavery which then existed in the Southern States." —Congressman Charles A. Lindbergh Sr. of Minnesota in *Banking and Currency, and the Money Trust,* National Capital Press, Washington, 1913, pp. 102-103.

"Not only is wealth accumulated, but immense power and despotic domination is concentrated in the hands of a few, and those few are frequently not the owners, but only the trustees and directors of invested funds, who administer them at pleasure. This power becomes particularly irresistible when exercised by those who, because they hold and control money, are able to govern credit and determine its allotment, thereby supplying life-blood to the entire economic body, and grasping in their hands the very soul of the economy so that nobody dare breathe against their will." —Pope Pius XI in parts 105 and 106 of the encyclical letter *Quadragesimo Anno,* published by the Holy See on May 15, 1931.

Contents

Foreword

National deficits, the Federal Reserve, and high finance rarely appear in discussions about the War Between the States. Battles, battlefields, military and political leaders, war diaries, or even cultural differences between the warring sides have received far more attention. When money is discussed, it is often treated in a predictable manner and centered on rising prices, taxes and tariffs, or destroyed properties. John Remington Graham moves financial matters forward in this carefully researched account, by going back in order to shed light on the present and to suggest remedies for correcting damage done to America's financial independence and solvency. Graham's father, who was a banker and economist, no doubt contributed to the author's interest in high finance. Such an interest, when combined with a passion for research and the skills of an experienced trial lawyer, gives him an advantage as he introduces neglected evidence.

The first time I read the manuscript, I had the eerie feeling I had seen similar material elsewhere. It reminded me of ideas I had noticed in the 1840s and 1850s novels of John Beauchamp Jones (1810-1866), in which Jones tirelessly and repeatedly connected government, business, and banking. Sometimes Jones cloaked money matters in mystery and treated them seriously. Other times he included money in situations so hilariously funny it was hard to remember money had even contributed to the comedy. My focus on J. B. Jones was literary and historical. When Graham looks at Jones, he is doing it from the point of view of business and banking, and in so doing Graham is doing, finally, what Jones spent his literary life insisting had to be done. Following the money.

As early as the 1840s, J. B. Jones was warning his readers to follow the money, to observe not only where it was going but where it had come from and what it was being used for. In book after book, Jones tried both to entertain and to educate readers who were lamentably unversed in emerging economic practices. Jones accurately predicted much of what actually took place throughout the country before, during, and after the War Between the States as he focused on the signs of growing civil unrest. Being savvy about matters of money, he knew how easily civil discord could be translated into dollar signs for those invested in conflict rather than peace.

When J. B. Jones died in 1866, the American Republic he so loved had already been dealt a death blow. The nation divided in war had not been stitched back together. Little more than clumsily applied bandages called peace wrapped the gaping wounds in the body politic. Would time heal the wounds, or would they fester?

In the ways of a good crime scene investigator, John Remington Graham has removed the bandages, exposed and examined the wounds, studied trace evidence still available in archives, and put his findings under a microscope now accessible to the public. Those who are convinced that the Republic established by the founding fathers has been dead and buried some generations ago may deem Graham's efforts as work on one very cold case indeed. These readers may doubt that Graham or anyone else could uncover any new clues. But they would be wrong. Graham has gone through layers deep inside the wounds to a place where he can do his best work. He has questioned the predictable suspects, among them the dark and shadowy figures of slavery, tariffs, and secession. His conclusion is that none of these usual suspects had the strength to deal the death blow to the American Republic. This point, I hasten to add, was also made by J. B. Jones.

How then do we bring closure to a cold case? Questioning the original suspects is part of it. So also is investigating media involvement. Did J. B. Jones suspect the media of improperly inciting the worst passions? Jones didn't have to suspect media involvement. He knew it existed. He was, after all, a journalist and newspaper editor who understood the media industry well and took it to task in several of his novels.

John Remington Graham calls into question the ethics of political figures of the period. J. B. Jones spared few politicians in his novels, and he was in a position to know them as few did. Jones was the editor of the *Madisonian* in 1842 during the Tyler administration. The *Madisonian* was President John Tyler's political mouthpiece. In fact, Jones dedicated *Freaks of Fortune* (1854) to a personal friend: "To Robert Tyler, Esq., who, with his father, retired from the presidential mansion—as they entered it—without fortune." In 1861, former President Tyler personally recommended J. B. Jones for a suitable position in the Confederacy.

Among the prized possessions Jones carried with him in his flight from New Jersey to Richmond was a "fine old portrait of Calhoun, by Jarvis." John C. Calhoun had offered Jones a post as *chargé d'affaires* in Naples during the Polk administration. Jones declined the position even though he respected the man offering it. As a quiet and introverted family man who had seen both the best and the worst of the inner workings of Washington, D.C., Jones was never inclined to seek or accept a political position. The very idea of using money as power disgusted him. The misuse of money in politics was irritating enough to find its way into Jones's novels.

Based on his experience and study, John Remington Graham shares Jones's assessment of bankers and lawyers during years leading up to the war. Some were moral, others were not. Few were incorruptible.

While J. B. Jones was a devout Christian and church-going Episcopalian, he never allowed clerical conduct of a questionable nature to slide past his pen. Preachers behaving badly were dealt with on the printed page in much the same way Jones doled out his scorn for radical abolitionists inciting crowds to riot. Graham actually goes easier on churchmen and abolitionists than Jones ever did. Did Jones know fiery-tongued preachers were stockpiling money in Northern churches? He did indeed, and turned the practice into one of his most entertaining and funny subplots.

In 1859 Jones pulled together various money pieces of the puzzle and sent to press a masterwork, *Border Wars: A Tale of Disunion,* later published as *Wild Southern Scenes,* then as *Secession, Coercion, and Civil War: The Story of 1861.* The work showed signs of eventually rivaling *Wild Western Scenes* (1841), Jones's first book, which had sold an amazing 100,000 copies over a twenty-year period. Actually, *Wild Western Scenes* kept soldiers on both sides of the war laughing as they pulled tattered copies from their packs and read from them on battlefields far from home.

The success of the last fiction Jones ever wrote was cut short when hostilities boiled over and hard fighting began. Jones had written about what might happen, but when what might happen actually became a terrible reality, even the most humorous aspects of the story lost their appeal. Reading about a potential disaster is one thing. Living with the real consequences is another. And Jones's sad tale of the reality that came about is recorded in his posthumously published *A Rebel War Clerk's Diary* (1866), to which Graham pays detailed attention in his text and notes.

If Graham's work has helped me to understand the message J. B. Jones was sending, then Jones's novels certainly prepared me to deal with the conclusions Graham reaches. The fatal wound that robbed the Republic of its life was neither slavery, nor tariffs, nor even secession. It was money, money bathed in the blood of American soldiers, both North and South.

I am reminded of all those Northerners who were beaten, hung, shot, or jailed—simply for protesting the invasion of the South. And I am reminded of all those Northerners who tried to help the South recover when the war was over. They too fought to defend a dying Republic which few—all too few—realized was being secretly stabbed in the back by those bent on making money out of its demise.

Born, educated, and called to the bar in Minnesota, John Remington Graham provides his readers with war-related information most Southerners will not know. As a son of Minnesota, for instance, Graham learned the legend and studied the life of Congressman Charles A. Lindbergh Sr. (1859-1924), whose observations in *Banking and Currency and the Money Trust* (1913) clearly link the Federal Reserve with the War Between the States. Lindbergh's work served as an inspiration to delve deeper. With the benefit of hindsight upon political and economic history, Graham also elaborates on material produced by the Iowa peace Democrat lawyer Henry Clay Dean (1822-1881) in *Crimes of the Civil War and Curse of the Funding System* (1868), and the engineer turned economist Alexander Del Mar (1836-1926) in *A History of Monetary Crimes* (1899). A multitude of statutes, important judicial decisions, legal rules of evidence and principles of inductive logic adapted to historical analysis, and Anglo-American constitutional law and history are all brought to bear on the subjects of war and money.

According to the sources used by Graham, the death of the American Republic, that shining light to oppressed humanity everywhere, was not caused by slavery. Nor was the death caused by unfair tariffs, or even by States asserting the right of secession. No, the great American experiment in constitutional government by the consent of the governed was ruined by a plot to gain control of banking and currency—the love of money, the root of all evil according to St. Paul. Blood money.

College of Charleston   DAVID AIKEN
December 22, 2005

Acknowledgments

I wish to thank Dr. Donald Livingston, founder and director of the Abbeville Institute, who enabled me to appreciate the historical writing of David Hume, and thereby weaned me once and for all from my youthful faith in "Whiggish" historians, so I might better understand Congressman Charles A. Lindbergh Sr., Minnesota's greatest statesman. Dr. Livingston challenged me to begin this work.

I wish to thank Dr. Clyde Wilson, devoted scholar of the statesman philosopher John C. Calhoun. Again and again Dr. Wilson obliged me to rethink and rewrite. And he introduced me to Henry Clay Dean, the incomparable peace Democrat from Iowa.

I wish to thank Roger Elletson, lawyer and educator, for introducing me to the work of the economist Alexander Del Mar whose penetrating insights into money as a medium of power inspired me in days when I protected farmers from predatory banking practices which my father had always abhorred and avoided.

I wish to thank Dr. David Aiken, master of Southern literature, who introduced me to the Civil War diarist J. B. Jones and guided me through maturing stages of this work.

I also wish to thank Dr. Marshall DeRosa, advocate and expounder of the Confederate States Constitution, for his review of my manuscript and his encouragement.

Thanks also to Tommy Curtis, ever loyal as a personal friend and Southern patriot, for acting as a sounding board and gentle prompter as I wrote and rewrote.

And I must not forget Dr. Milburn Calhoun who patiently sent me back to my desk several times for better exploitation of the possibilities in my text and notes. —J. R. G.

An Important Insight Reexamined

From 1861 to 1865, the Southern States were conquered by an overwhelming military assault which deeply injured the economy and culture of the region. This assault is usually called the American Civil War, for it was not unlike the war between the Cavaliers and Roundheads at the time of Charles the First. The struggle is also called the War Between the States, because it was a war between a Union of Northern States and a Confederacy of Southern States, or the War for Southern Independence, because it distinctly resembled the American Revolution.

The surrender of the last rebel armies was followed by a long period of reconstruction during which Southern representatives and senators were excluded from Congress, and constitutional government was abolished in ten of the former Confederate States. The vast majority of white citizens were disenfranchised, and military occupation and martial law were imposed upon the defeated people of those States. An unhappy postbellum age of lawlessness, corruption, and oppression lingered until the last Federal troops were finally withdrawn from Louisiana in 1877.

This discourse will reconsider a view of the American Civil War associated with such names as Henry Clay Dean, J. B. Jones, Alexander Del Mar, and Charles A. Lindbergh Sr. These remarkable observers, each in his own way, contributed to a bold and terrible thesis, which may thus be restated:

The divisive antagonisms between the North and the South, finally erupting in the spring of 1861, were not unfortunate historical accidents, nor the result of some inexorable momentum in events. Those antagonisms, rather, were deliberately agitated during the 1850s by great international banking houses with a preconceived motive of provoking secession. And secession was to be used as a pretext for a bloody and expensive war of conquest, which was actually launched and carried out. The war was planned as a brutal slaughter, as it tragically became. The war was planned to generate a stupendous national debt, mostly represented by bonds, and such a national debt was in fact generated. The private interests acquiring these bonds successfully plotted to secure the passage of legislation which enabled them to convert the paper by them acquired in financing the war into a new and dominant system of banking and currency under their ownership and control. And those private interests fully succeeded in their sinister program, and set up a huge financial empire centered on Wall Street from which they have ever since governed the United States from behind the scenes.

Henry Clay Dean was a lawyer living in Iowa during the war. He personally witnessed the heart-sickening events of those days. He was falsely arrested and imprisoned without trial, suffering serious injury to his health, because he detected the gigantic fraud and corruption which propelled the war, and warned his fellow citizens what was afoot. As a peace Democrat, he had considerable stature in those troubled times. "The capitalists and stock gamblers in Europe," he said, "by their alliance with the political adventurers of America, carefully planned this war in the interest of despotism and the funding systems. They anticipated every argument, and prepared the public mind for war in advance. During the war they prepared for the debt and continued the war that the debt might reach its present enormous extent."[1] From figures then published, Dean reckoned that by 1866 the war had caused the public debt of the United States to multiply by more than fifty-three times the amount due in 1860. The magnitude of this growth in public debt can be gauged by the fact that the principal due in 1860 was about equal in specie to the public debt of the United States as reckoned in 1791. Thus the public debt generated by the American Civil War each month substantially exceeded the entire public debt generated by the American Revolution. By 1866, the public debt of the United States had grown until it was about equal to the public debt of the British Empire, which did not come from fighting one war lasting a few years, but had accumulated from fighting many wars following the incorporation of the Bank of England in 1694. And the interest paid on this vastly augmented public debt of the United States in 1866 much exceeded all other appropriations by Congress, and was twice the interest paid on public debt by Great Britain.[2]

This consummation was dangerous, not only because of the horrendous weight of the burden imposed, but even more because it concentrated in the hands of a coterie of great financiers for their own benefit, without regard to the public good, virtually unchecked discretion to expand and contract the supply of money, currency, and deposits functioning as money. It gave them practical means to alter the flow or availability of money and credit, and thus to stimulate or enfeeble at pleasure any activity which requires money and credit, be it manufacturing, industry, agriculture, commerce, education, scholarship, culture, art, music, or even religion. It enabled them to induce changes in prices on the market, so they might buy when prices fell, sell when prices rose, and thereby take windfall profits. It conferred discretion to exploit according to preconceived but secret plans by expanding credit to stimulate economic activity of one kind or another, then terminating or diminishing credit, thereby causing unanticipated reversals in fortune unrelated to the natural fluctuations of the free market, allowing lenders to acquire property by foreclosures and money judgments. It gave them privileged access to the halls of government, —the opportunity to buy and sell politicians with impunity. It gave them the capacity to finance political campaigns of their favorites, to acquire dominance in the news media, and thereby to sway most elections. Control of nearly all domestic and foreign policy of the government followed as a matter of course. These private interests, therefore, became more powerful than the lawful government of the land. They became de facto an "invisible government" of the United States.

Therefore, the most important consequence of the American Civil War was loss of the monetary independence of the United States. And that, as a practical matter, was also loss of political independence behind a façade of "freedom" and "democracy."

It will do no harm to qualify our thesis, lest needless apprehensions result. Great financiers cannot be identified as the only culprits behind the American Civil War. For that overstates the case, and attributes to them means and influence more pervasive than they actually had. Pseudo-religious fanaticism, raw greed and corruption, political folly, unwholesome ambition, and cultural misunderstanding were abundant in those days. But such evils have been troublesome in almost every age. While problems then festering had particularly interesting features, war could easily have been avoided. And unless events had been cunningly manipulated by interests with sufficient capital to exaggerate destructive personalities and influences all out of proportion to their actual importance, the generation living in 1860 would have come and gone without major incident.

The Questions of Secession and Slavery

The American Civil War has been justified by a standard line of propaganda as a gallant crusade to save the Union and free the slaves. And so attention has been distracted from the hard reality of taking over banking

and currency by debate over whether the Southern States had a constitutional right to secede from the Union, and whether military conquest was
a moral necessity to abolish slavery. A few observations will help put these
questions in perspective.

Never was there a stronger secession movement in the United States
than in New England during the War of 1812. The particulars are laid out
clearly enough in the Journal and Report of the Hartford Convention,[3]
which met at the end of 1814 and adjourned in early 1815 to protest
against an unjust and unnecessary war imposed by Southern politicians
upon the commercial section of the Union. For New England desired
peace and trade with Great Britain and Canada. Secession from the Union
was actually contemplated. Breakup of the Union was avoided because
President James Madison saw the danger before the situation degenerated
too far, and successfully negotiated the Treaty of Ghent.

Leading antebellum text writers on the United States Constitution in
the North and the South had no difficulty in conceding a constitutional
right of the several States to secede from the Union. St. George Tucker,
Professor of Law at the College of William and Mary, and Justice of the
Virginia Supreme Court, prepared an annotated edition of Blackstone's
Commentaries on the Laws of England, published by Birch & Small of
Philadelphia in 1803, and widely used by the legal profession in the
United States. In Appendix D in the first volume of his edition, on page
187, Judge Tucker concluded that each State of the Union is "still sover-
eign, still independent, and still capable, should the situation require, to
resume the exercise of its functions in the most unlimited extent." The
same right of secession was expounded by William Rawles, appointed by
President George Washington as United States Attorney in Pennsylvania,
in his *View of the Constitution of the United States,* first edition published by
Carey & Lea of Philadelphia in 1825, second edition published by Philip
Nicklin of Philadelphia in 1829. In the last chapter of both editions,
Rawles concluded that any State "may wholly withdraw from the
Union." This text was used for instruction at West Point, and it was
highly recommended for professional and scholarly use as late as 1859.

Many Northern newspapers editorialized in 1860 and 1861 that the
Southern States should be allowed to withdraw from the Union in peace.[4] In
less than two weeks after the election of Abraham Lincoln as President of the
United States, the *Cincinnati Daily Press* trumpeted, "We believe that the
right of any member of this Confederacy to dissolve its political relations
with the others and assume an independent position is absolute." Particularly

striking were editorials soon following in New York City.[5] "If the cotton States decide they can do better out of the Union," said the *New York Tribune,* "we insist on letting them go in peace. The right to secede may be a revolutionary right, but it exists nevertheless." And the *New York Herald* added, "Each State is organized as a complete government, possessing the right to break the tie of the Confederation. Coercion, if it were possible, is out of the question." The day after Jefferson Davis was inaugurated provisional President of the Confederate States, the *Detroit Free Press* editorialized, "An attempt to subjugate the seceded States, even if successful, could produce nothing but evil, —evil unmitigated in character, and appalling in extent." A month later, the *New York Times* observed, "There is a growing sentiment throughout the North in favor of letting the Gulf States go."

In view of this respectable political sentiment, well founded in legal scholarship, it is impossible to make a fair argument that the war was caused by secession in 1860 and 1861. Both sides agreed that secession from the Union was reserved to the several States, and a war cannot be fought over a question on which both sides agree.

For that matter, peaceful secession of the Southern States would probably have been in the best interests of all concerned, for power would be more prudently distributed across North America today, if the Confederate States, the United States, and the Dominion of Canada occupied the continental expanse above the Rio Grande. Each confederacy would then protect the traditions and culture of a distinct civilization, yet all three unions could interact productively by treaties of commerce and alliance, while counterbalancing each other from excess. So the war was not necessary to maintain sound continental order. On the contrary, the breakup of the United States was certainly foreseen in the Philadelphia Convention as a natural and inevitable event. For Nathaniel Gorham of Massachusetts had served as President of Congress under the Articles of Confederation, and as Chairman of the Committee of the Whole in the Philadelphia Convention. And to emphasize the obvious, Gorham casually asked a rhetorical question during deliberations on August 7, 1787: "Can it be supposed that this vast country, including the western territory, will one hundred fifty years hence be one nation?"[6]

Nor does it make sense to argue that slavery was a cause of the war. The subject has become delicate because of irresponsible attempts to characterize relics of the War for Southern Independence as symbols of racism, oppression, and hatred. Yet the only really significant antebellum movement to abolish slavery generated in the Southern States. And this movement, fathered by Thomas Jefferson and fostered by James Madison, was highly prestigious and influential.

By contrast, the abolition movement in the North became so enfeebled by pathetic eccentricity that it had to be reinvigorated by James Birney of Alabama who, after freeing his slaves, twice ran for President on a platform calling for an end to slavery throughout the United States.[7]

Nowhere in any of the Northern States during the antebellum period was there ever a debate over slavery so distinguished, so important, and so eloquent as was held during the proceedings of the Virginia House of Delegates in 1832. The often magnificent speeches in this debate were published by newspapers in Richmond at the time, and have since been conveniently preserved for interested scholars.[8] Noteworthy about these proceedings is the fact that Southern abolitionists were dominant and carried important votes. It will be instructive to consider one speaker whose words are fairly illustrative of the oratorical offerings which then rang in legislative halls. On the tenth day of the debate, the Southern abolitionist James McDowell unforgettably expounded the fundamental error of slavery:

> "Sir, you may place the slave where you please. You may dry up, to your utmost, the foundations of his feeling, the springs of his thought. You may close his mind to every avenue of knowledge and cloud it over with artificial night. You may yoke him to your labours as the ox which liveth only to work and worketh only to live. You may put him under any process which, without destroying his value as a slave, will debase and crush him as a rational being. You may do all this, and the idea that he was born to be free will survive it all. It is allied to his hope of immortality. It is the ethereal part of his nature which oppression cannot reach."

Yet in the same speech, McDowell reported a truth about slavery as practiced in the Old South, as he knew from personal observation, because, in his legislative district slaves made up 26% of the population. McDowell said:

> "It is true, sir, to the letter, what gentlemen have frequently declared, that there is no laboring peasantry in any other part of the world, who, in all external respects, are better situated than our slave, —who suffers less from want, who suffers less from hardship, who struggles less under the toils of life, and or who has a fuller supply of the comforts which mere physical nature demands. In all these respects he shares the equalizing and benignant spirit of our institutions and our age. He is not the victim of cruelty. He is rarely, if ever, harmed by oppression. He is governed by an

authority which year after year is abating of its harshness, and is admitted to every privilege which the deprivation of his liberty can allow."

McDowell later served as Governor of Virginia (1843-1846). He and other abolitionists in the Virginia House of Delegates agreed that slavery ran against natural law, yet was not cruel or oppressive. In the wake of propaganda peddled over more than a century to justify the American Civil War, it has generally been believed that slavery was a harsh system, but in time lies lose their force, and eventually comparisons are made between irresponsible claims and the actual facts. It has now been demonstrated with hard economic data that the slaves of the Old South fared much better than factory workers in the North with respect to health, diet, leisure, longevity, and general well-being.[9] The bad consequences of slavery were not what could be appreciated by abstractionists in the North who had no touch with reality. McDowell explained the faults of slavery in his observation "that the slaveholding interest of the country will and can coalesce with no other interest," and "must be hostile to all others." Slavery was wrong, not because it was brutal and hard, which it was certainly not, but because it robbed society of vitality and energy. This opinion was shared by most people of Virginia in 1832, and their House of Delegates passed a resolution which lamented "the great evils arising from the condition of the colored population of the commonwealth." Southern abolitionists made no further progress at that juncture, only because there was great uncertainty on how to proceed.

If today the country were confronted with a giant and entrenched system of workfare, in which a very large segment of the labor force had been subordinated over many generations to work on certain projects and was compensated in kind rather than in money—and such was pretty much the nature of slavery in the Old South—, serious reformers would not suggest immediate and sweeping abolition. For serious reformers would approach the problem by careful planning to phase out the system gradually, enabling those affected to adjust and find jobs, while seeking to discover ways to assure an adequate work force for projects served by the old system to the extent such projects were still necessary for society. But even then opinion would be divided over exactly how to rid society of the blight.

In one of his noted speeches before the war,[10] Abraham Lincoln himself said of slavery, "If all earthly power were given to me, I should not know what to do as to the existing institution." He did not know what to do, because nobody really knew how to make abolition humane, practical, and beneficial. There were many contradictions produced by slavery, and Lincoln himself conceded them. The Virginia statesman John Randolph of Roanoke left a will freeing his slaves, and established a trust to buy land for them in the free State of Ohio so they could survive and prosper, but the people in the free State of Ohio drove the freedmen from the farms which their Southern champion had procured for them.[11]

During the war, it was widely believed in the Southern States that general emancipation of all slaves was sure to come not long following independence.[12] As Union armies approached Richmond, slaves living in the city reacted, not in happy anticipation of freedom, but in fear of losing all they had. Across the Southern States, slaves energetically built breastworks and fortifications to defend their homeland. Thousands of black troops fought for Southern independence, and saw combat. Robert E. Lee, who had freed hundreds of slaves before the war as executor of his father-in-law's estate, was himself regarded by his fellow Southerners as favoring general emancipation of all slaves. With the support of most officers and men in Confederate armies, General Lee proposed enlistment of slaves with freedom as a bounty, such as had been a frequent practice during the American Revolution. The Southern Congress eventually authorized the plan by law. And President Davis implemented the plan with executive regulations.

Certainly the war did not bring about a humane, practical, and beneficial transformation from servitude to freedom. William Sharkey was one of the most enlightened patriots of the Old South. In 1852, he became Chief Justice of Mississippi. At the conclusion of hostilities in 1865, he became reconstruction governor of his State under President Andrew Johnson, and in that capacity he led the people of Mississippi in convention to abolish slavery before the 13th Amendment was adopted. In testimony given before Congress,[13] Judge Sharkey described the devastating impact which the "armies of freedom" and the "great emancipator" had upon the black race:

> "I believe that there are now in my State very little over half the number of freedmen that were formerly slaves, certainly not more than two-thirds. They have died off. There is no telling the mortality that has prevailed among them; they have died off in immense numbers. I should say that very little more than half the amount of land that was under cultivation before the war will be under cultivation this year."

Once confined by geography to certain limits, slavery was a doomed institution. It was doomed, because it was quasi-feudal, and the South also underwent a rapid process of modernization. The culture of the

South enabled the region to adapt more gracefully to the emergence of railroads, telegraph, larger cities, industry, machinery, and invention, but nothing could dilute the rapid obsolescence of slavery, —nothing except, perhaps, expansion of the institution into new territory suited to the planter way of life. Nor was this fact unknown to Southerners.

It has been said that the institution might have continued at least in the slave States had Southern whites been determined to maintain it. Yet Southern whites were not determined to maintain it. The institution was still tolerated only because Southerners knew that sudden uprooting would cause more problems than it would solve. If slaves might conceivably have been used in the mines of the Southwest, nobody in the Dixie States was inclined to make an attempt. Hence in 1860 Congressman Otho Singleton of Mississippi made this striking concession: "I ask again, what will be the future of the Southern slaveholder? If slavery be confined to its present limits, the institution will necessarily be overthrown. It is only a matter of time."[14]

In 1860 there was no real possibility that slavery could or would expand into the Federal territories. The reasons, based on geography and modernization, are plainly enough laid out by Charles Ramsdell in his classic article, *The Natural Limits of Slavery Expansion,* 16 Mississippi Valley Historical Review 151-171 (1929). In all of the Federal territories in 1860, there were not many thousands of slaves as commonly assumed, not even many hundreds. Nor were planters in the Dixie States interested in moving west, although they were free by law to do so. There were in those days exactly seventeen slaves in all the Federal territories, two of them in Kansas, which entered the Union the next year without slavery, and none of them in any of the territories eventually claimed by the Confederate States. Following the Virginia slavery debates, natural processes began to nudge slavery into ultimate extinction. By 1860, these processes were in full motion. Nothing more was needed than cautious prudence, artful legislation, and wise statesmanship to usher the institution into the mists of the past within the course of fifty years.

A Conspiratorial View of History

Why, then, the War Between the States? There was no moral or economic justification which could be built upon hard facts. There were no unstoppable forces which made secession inevitable or even desirable. Still less was there any just cause or urgent reason which made war necessary to counteract secession. In more tranquil circumstances, secession could easily enough have been avoided, and adjustments between the North and South might have been accomplished within the Union. Nor is there any reason why the North and South could not have existed as neighboring federal structures in peace and friendship.

Yet popular opinion and vulgar passions had been whipped up by the Presidential election in 1860 to such a pitch that the country was waiting to explode in consequence of a few awkward political mistakes. Sensitive questions had been cunningly agitated during the 1850s until the public mind was dangerously inflamed. These questions had been agitated to provoke a frightfully bloody and expensive civil war, and thereby to run up a huge national debt which could be used as a vehicle for taking over banking and currency in the United States.

It is initially hard to accept such a conspiratorial view, because we have been conditioned to a "Whiggish" theory of history which says that key events occur because of broad forces and trends over time, that these broad forces and trends eventually assume foreseeable patterns from their own inertia, and that by means of these patterns history marches inexorably toward a triumph of freedom over oppression and science over ignorance, etc. This rosy view of things tells us that the French Revolution, to take a particularly instructive example, happened because of broad forces and trends of history, and really was for the good of mankind. In France, we are told, the noblesse had long been untaxed, the church had long been corrupt, the people had long been oppressed, and the constitution of the kingdom had become irreparably demented. Great excitement was felt when French troops returned from America after Yorktown, we are told. The situation was exceedingly tense, the argument goes. And so when King Louis XVI offered hope of reform, it was impossible to have an orderly and beneficial process. Instead, the goddess of liberty, carrying a musket in one hand and a tricolor in the other, led the people to claim their just rights! Revolution, judicial murder, genocide, wars, and political chaos became inevitable. This view does not add up, and the picture it draws does not hang together, yet it is the fare usually offered and swallowed.

More insightful historians such as John Robison[15] and Nesta Webster,[16] not to mention a number of good French writers, have understood that the French Revolution was not and could not have been a spontaneous event. It happened because men, some of them evil, some of them deluded, planned it on a grand scale and carried out their designs. In fact, Louis XVI was a good man, eminent among the founding fathers of the United States, and father of the French people whom he conscientiously consulted in framing constitutional reforms which he intended to see implemented. As a whole the nation believed that the government should remain a monarchy, that the Crown was hereditary from male to male, that the King was inviolable and sacred, that royal sanction was necessary for promulgation of laws, and that the constitution should be reformed after the British model, only adapted to the particular circumstances of France. There was no popular desire for an uprising or even a republic. Nor was progress obstructed by the noblesse and the clergy, who, on the contrary, were anxious to promote meaningful constitutional reform. The revolution was excited by ruthless subversives in the third estate—the likes of Robespierre, Danton, and St-Just, even the prostitute illuminatus Mirabeau was among them—, and by the fifth Duc d'Orléans or "Philippe Égalité" who was duped, used, then sent to the guillotine.

The American Civil War likewise would not have happened if it had not been planned and fomented.

Consider John Brown's raid on Harper's Ferry in 1859, which became a political powder keg and later a rationalization for war crimes. In late 1864, for example, as Atlanta burned, and women and children were sent homeless onto the countryside, the military band of Sherman's army jubilantly played "John Brown's Body." It is naïve to suppose that Brown's raid was caused by broad forces and trends in history. The fugitive slave law then on the books was artless. But John Brown could not on his own have mounted his raid because a few people were upset about a bad law which, in any event, was seldom used. It would have been possible to introduce better legislation in Congress, and Southern representatives and senators could have been found to support it. John Brown had no mass appeal even in the North. He could have done nothing if he had not been financed by a coterie of wealthy individuals who conspired to promote his designs. It is not necessary to have the details to know that there must have been some such conspiracy, probably centered in New England, supporting and financing John Brown. At the time, not a few sensed some such plot. And contemporary scholarship has identified the particulars of exactly such a combination.[17]

The details are interesting, in part because they satisfy natural curiosity concerning the individuals, their personalities, and their circumstances. The details are even more interesting in that they illustrate how and why otherwise good citizens, honored in their communities—two reverend clergymen, two wealthy businessmen, a distinguished educator, and a respected physician, themselves encouraged by famous poets and scholars—, could be and were induced to hire a vicious murderer and a gang of outlaws who, as they knew, would commit hideous acts of homicide and arson against their own countrymen in a neighboring State. The first to die in Brown's raid to free black slaves was a freed black, and from this beginning a multitude of ironies follow, one after another until the whole affair can be seen as profoundly stupid. The conspirators fully understood that Brown was a con artist and thug with pathological tendencies. They knew of the brutal and inhuman crimes which he had earlier committed in the Kansas Territory. They knew also that Brown's uprising would almost certainly fail, that Brown himself would surely hang for treason, and that the episode might well ignite a fratricidal war, thereby threatening civilized legal order on the continent.

The details are especially interesting in that they confirm the reality of a conspiracy which natural reason tells us must have been formed and carried out, but from which we recoil because the very thought is so repugnant. The details provide a wholesome sense of confidence in insights that certain distinctive patterns in events must have been orchestrated by human design.

John Brown's raid was a microcosm of the age in which he lived. The combination behind him was a conspiracy within a conspiracy, a scenario within a scenario. The attempt to make Brown a martyr was not the insanity of an individual, but an act of collective insanity. And if the episode is so understood, it is not quite so difficult to comprehend the plans of great banking houses to cause a fraternal bloodbath with a view to gaining control over the money and credit in the United States.

The difficulty in grasping such a reality derives from assumptions commonly entertained by historians as they interpret events falling within their discipline. Even if unconsciously, they want to believe in the seductive heresy of Pelagius who lived in the 5th Century and taught that the original sin, if ever committed, was never transmitted to later generations, and that man is naturally good. But authentic Christianity has always taught that man is a fallen creature in need of redemption, that sinfulness is inherent in human nature, and that evil is an active force in the universe. Working from this premise, Christianity has been able to establish Western civilization with a remarkable degree of success, as by building huge Gothic cathedrals to sap up energy that otherwise would have been devoted to war, while inspiring men and women to rise above their humanity into sainthood.

By contrast the philosophy of the "enlightenment" was that human nature is naturally good, and that the church and crown prevented the manifestation of goodness. And this ideology motivated the conspiracies which produced the French Revolution. Yet the mass executions of patriots and innocents in Paris as mobs chanted cheap slogans, the patricide and matricide which inflicted deep wounds in the soul of France still not healed, the genocide in the Vendée, and the wars of Napoleon, are all a powerful demonstration that the revolution was founded upon a dangerous error. And this same philosophy of the enlightenment bewitches us into believing that the American Civil War must have been fought for good ends, which is the furthest thing from the truth.

It is commonly argued by sceptics that the evidence is insufficient to "prove" this or that combination, as if circumstantial evidence were inferior to direct evidence. But, whatever historians may think, the law has learned from experience over long centuries that circumstantial evidence is frequently better than direct evidence. Circumstantial evidence is necessary and often sufficient when no direct evidence is available. Circumstantial evidence sometimes provides clarity when direct evidence is ambiguous, for an indisputable fact can settle a question when eyewitnesses do not know or cannot agree. Circumstantial evidence is usually adventitious, and therefore difficult to fabricate or impeach, whereas direct evidence is often impaired by prevarication, perjury, or mistake. Cross-examination can expose a lying witness, but is powerless against a telling fact. If intuition supported by circumstantial evidence were insufficient in court, the law would make little progress in seeking justice.

If an historian must exclude everything but direct evidence before he fashions a definitive thesis, his vision will be reduced to inconclusive particulars. It is unrealistic, in any event, to expect that, in uncovering a conspiracy to take over banking and currency in the United States, we might find a transcript made from shorthand notes taken by a private secretary of a secret conversation among international financiers in one of the great banking house of Europe. Nor do we need such evidence to deepen our understanding of the American Civil War.

The Rules of Evidence

In order to stimulate a civil war within the United States, it was necessary to foment hatred between the North and the South. And in order to appreciate the reality of such a conspiracy, it is important to appreciate a few practical rules of evidence. The first rule is actually a

sagacious and indispensable rule of law on which juries have traditional-
ly been instructed from the bench: men are presumed in law to have
intended the natural and foreseeable consequences of their own acts.

The other rule is really rooted in a principle of inductive logic
called Ockham's razor, which was stated in so many words by Sir Isaac
Newton at the beginning of the third book of his *Principia:* given a
distinctive pattern or tendency in events, assign the simplest and most
fitting explanation as the cause, unless and until another more reasonable and plausible explanation later appears from new evidence. This
rule was originally framed to deal with philosophical questions concerning universals and relations. It was expanded by Newton to
explain the movements of heavenly bodies, and is properly used today
in all the empirical sciences. It may be used even in politics and law.
With this important principle in mind, it is easier to appreciate an
unforgettable observation by Abraham Lincoln in his famous "House
Divided" speech[18] given on the occasion of his nomination by the
Republican Party in Illinois as a candidate for United States Senate:

> "We cannot absolutely know that all these exact adaptations are the
> result of preconcert. But when we see a lot of framed timbers, different
> portions of which we know have been gotten at different times and places
> by different workmen—Stephen, Franklin, Roger, and James, for
> instance—, and when we see these timbers joined together, and see they
> exactly make the frame of a house or a mill, all the tenons and mortices
> exactly fitting, and all the lengths and proportions of the different pieces
> exactly adapted to their respective places, and not a piece too many or too
> few—not omitting even scaffolding—or, if a single piece be lacking, we
> see the place in the frame exactly fitted and prepared yet to bring such
> piece in, —in such a case, we find it impossible not to believe that
> Stephen and Franklin and Roger and James all understood one another
> from the beginning, and all worked upon a common plan or draft drawn
> up before the first blow was struck."

When Lincoln made this comment, he spoke as a seasoned trial lawyer.
He meant that, if events are of a kind which ordinarily would not happen unless men plotted to advance a certain objective, then we should not
be inundated with doubt, but may and should confidently postulate a
conspiracy to accomplish that objective. There is actually such a judicial
standard for proving up conspiracy in civil litigation, once aptly
expressed as follows:[19]

"Conspirators do not make minutes of their machinations, progress, and objectives. Seldom, therefore, can conspiracy be proved by other than circumstantial evidence. It is only by assembling the results, with such evidence as may be of the progress thereof by the participants, that the victim can ever make a case of conspiracy. If in the end there is a completed structure of result, the frame of which has been furnished piecemeal by several individuals, the parts when brought together showing adaptation to each other and fitness for the end accomplished, it is at least reasonable to infer concert in both planning and fabrication."

When Lincoln delivered his "House Divided" speech, he believed or at least said that events of his day were shaped by powerful men with an agenda to expand and perpetuate slavery. His logic was correct, but he argued his case on incomplete evidence. There was a conspiracy afoot, but not of Southern planters seeking to bring slavery into the Federal territories where slavery was prohibited by geography. It was instead a combination of great financiers, and their agenda was to generate a war that would help them take over banking and currency in the United States.

In what follows, the rules of natural reason just explained will be assumed in discussing events so they may be seen in a clearer light. The distinctive features of the analysis following will in part rest on evidence not previously considered with sufficient attention, but will turn more largely on an awakened understanding of how events should be interpreted.

Inciting Hatred: Uncle Tom's Cabin

The opening salvo in the campaign to sow hatred was Harriet Beecher Stowe's *Uncle Tom's Cabin,* first serialized in a newspaper, then published as a book in 1852. It was not a reasoned argument against slavery. It had no basis in fact. It was pure fiction, reaching a melodramatic climax in a scene where the sadistic master Simon Legree murders a kindly slave Uncle Tom who pleads, "Mas'r, if you was sick, or in trouble, or dying, and I could save ye, I'd give ye my heart's blood; and, if taking every drop of blood in this poor old body would save your precious soul, I'd give 'em freely, as the Lord gave his for me. O, Mas'r, don't bring this great sin on your soul!" After more gaudy sensationalism, the awful moment arrived: "There was one hesitating pause, —one irresolute, relenting thrill, —and the spirit of evil came back, with sevenfold vehemence; and Legree, foaming with rage, smote his victim to the ground."

This vindictive fabrication was published as a malicious libel against the Old South. It was mass marketed, requiring vast capital which could only have been supplied by the largest banking houses in the United States and Great Britain. This book was promoted lavishly, like no other book ever before promoted in the history of Western civilization. The King James Bible and the Book of Common Prayer aside, ten times more copies were published and sold than of any other work then known in the English-speaking world.[20] Mrs. Stowe's corny novel could not have gained a large readership without the kind of advertising and fanfare that only powerful connections and big money could assure. Pushing her work was like selling a low-grade Hollywood film today. It might be tasteless, as so many films are, but with enough capital it is possible to sell almost anything. Northerners read Mrs. Stowe's absurdity, and were outraged because they believed it was true. Southerners read her lie, and were outraged because they knew it was false. There was enough resulting anger in the air to generate the desire in men to kill each other, an essential ingredient of war, —exactly what the financiers behind this "literary" production wanted.

Transcontinental Railroads and the Repeal of the Missouri Compromise

Next came legislative adjustments in the Federal territories concerning the institution of slavery.

In 1820 Missouri was admitted into the Union. The new State lay to the west of the Mississippi River. On the other side of that great water-way, the Ohio River and the Mason-Dixon Line distinguished the modern industrialized society in the Northern States from the quasi-feudal agrarian society in the Southern States. While the two cultures could exist side by side on the same continental expanse, they could never be mixed, because each civilization was radically different from the other. Human beings are remarkably territorial. They will fight and kill for land to maintain a particular way of life.

If the latitude of the confluence of the Ohio and Mississippi Rivers were extended in a westerly direction as a continuing boundary between the Northern and Southern States, Missouri should have come into the Union without slavery. Yet, because the planter way of life was well entrenched in Missouri when she applied for admission to the Union, it was wholly impractical to prohibit slavery in the new State.

Legislators from Northern States wanted to be sure that they would get a good piece of the Federal territories. It was not altruism, but a desire to preserve an adequate domain for their civilization that prompted this desire. They were indifferent to slavery as a moral question, but they knew that, if the institution were firmly implanted anywhere, it would be more difficult to implant their way of life in that place.

Under the guidance of Henry Clay, an accommodation was reached to allow the new State with slavery. The deal extended the southern boundary of Missouri, which was at 36 degrees 30 minutes north latitude, in a westerly direction, cutting the Federal territories in two parts. Below that line were Indian lands, or Oklahoma, and what became Texas upon her admission to the Union some years later, and there slavery was allowed by law. Above that line was then-unorganized territory, a major part of the Louisiana Purchase transacted in 1803, and there slavery was prohibited by law. In that unorganized territory just to the west of Missouri lay what later became Kansas, and to the north and west lay what later became Nebraska.

This "Missouri Compromise" or Compromise of 1820[21] was considered by statesmen of the country as a solemn pact between the North and the South, enabling the two civilizations to coexist within the same Union.

Again under the guidance of Henry Clay, the Compromise of 1850[22] was reached to deal with the expanse of continent ceded two years earlier by Mexico to the United States. This legislation did not formally prohibit slavery in the new Federal territories, nor was such an interdiction necessary, because geography made it impossible to implant slavery to the south and west of the Nueces River in Texas, or into or beyond Oklahoma, or upon any part of the land acquired from Mexico.

Aging patriots made these arrangements to save the Union. The great ones among them—Henry Clay, Daniel Webster, and John Calhoun—died by the end of 1852, and slavery began to pass into the mists of history. All that was needed was the quiet passing of time. The inflammatory language of *Uncle Tom's Cabin* stirred up passions, but even that baneful influence was not enough to prevent the Compromises of 1820 and 1850 from doing their merciful work, if only they remained untouched.

But they were not left untouched. And the meddling hands, as with *Uncle Tom's Cabin,* were again the hands of large banking houses, this time financing a grand transcontinental railroad, from the eastern end at Chicago through Iowa, then across the unorganized territory to the north and west of Missouri, and from San Francisco on the Pacific coast across territory ceded by Mexico, until the two projects joined in Utah.[23] The difficulty was that the South offered and wanted a shorter route from New Orleans through Texas, thence by the Gila Valley to San Diego. Stephen Douglas, Chairman of the Committee on Territories in the United States Senate, was ambitious to become President, and was supported in his ambition by the financiers behind the central route from Chicago to San Francisco. As a quid pro quo, Douglas supported the central route which those financiers wanted. In order to buy off enough Southern votes to get the central route, Douglas secured passage of the Kansas-Nebraska Act in 1854.[24] This legislation established the Kansas Territory and the Nebraska Territory, and included a provision repealing the prohibition of slavery in the Louisiana Purchase above 36 degrees 30 minutes north latitude as ordained by the Missouri Compromise.[25]

There were great Southerners who opposed this sale of the Missouri Compromise to suit the demands of political ambition, railroad building, and high finance. Among them was Sam Houston of Texas. But enough Southerners went along, including some good men who did not appreciate the magnitude of the blunder. The repeal meant that the Kansas Territory, directly to the west of Missouri, was open to settlement both to people from the North, with their way of life, and people from the South, with their way of life. In the bulk of the Federal territories, such a possibility really would not matter, because the climate and terrain generally did not welcome slavery. But there was one exception, of all places within the Kansas Territory: in a small region along the Kansas and Missouri Rivers, hemp and tobacco might have been profitably grown and harvested by slave labor.

That was enough to bring people from both the North and the South into the Kansas Territory. As night follows day, a civil war broke out between the two populations in 1855, and it continued on and off over several years. Hatred had been incited by large banking houses financing libel, and a battleground had been arranged by large banking houses financing a railroad. The hostilities erupting in the new territory were a kind of dress rehearsal for the big event coming up.

A lot of howling and posturing over "Bleeding Kansas" was stirred up by Salmon P. Chase of Ohio and Charles Sumner of Massachusetts in the United States Senate. Both of them were closely allied to Northern railroad, industrial, and financial interests, for it was practically impossible for anybody in the United States Senate from a State above the Mason Dixon Line and the Ohio River not to have "conversations" with individuals representing such powerful concerns. But in spite of Chase and Sumner, the trouble in the Kansas Territory was settled, and out of it came a new State admitted to the Union without slavery in 1861. The most interesting feature of this episode is that it was, not the likes of Chase and Sumner, but Southern statesmen, who caused the fighting to end in the Kansas Territory. It was these Southern statesmen who caused peaceful voting to occur, votes to be honestly counted, and a new free State to enter the Union. They included especially Robert Toombs of Georgia in the United States Senate, and territorial governors Robert Walker of Mississippi and Frederick Stanton of Tennessee.

The Case of Dred Scott

As troubles in the Kansas Territory continued, a fateful case arose before the United States Supreme Court. Some background concerning this litigation will be in order here.

In 1834 an army surgeon, John Emerson, MD, took his slave Dred Scott on a tour of duty to Fort Snelling, then part of the Wisconsin Territory within the limits of the Louisiana Purchase where slavery had been prohibited by the Missouri Compromise. While at Fort Snelling, Scott married a female slave named Harriet whom Dr. Emerson had purchased from an army officer there stationed. From this union two daughters, Eliza and Lizzie, were born.

Some years later, after the death of his master whom he loved, Dred Scott sued Dr. Emerson's heir and widow before the circuit court of Missouri, seeking title to his freedom, and the freedom of his wife and daughters. Scott's case was open and shut.

For in *Rachael v. Walker*, 4 Mo. 350 at 351-354 (1836), the Missouri Supreme Court had held that, when even a military officer of the United States took his slave into territory made free by the Missouri Compromise, there to reside during a tour of duty, the slave became forever free, and was entitled to judgment accordingly. That case was based on previous decisions of the Missouri Supreme Court going back to the earliest days of statehood, in which slaves were adjudged forever free after their masters took them to reside where slavery was prohibited by the Northwest Ordinance of 1787,[26] or by the constitutions of States formed out of the Northwest Territory. These decisions of the Missouri Supreme Court were like countless others handed down by eminent judges and high courts throughout the South.[27] During the antebellum period, more slaves were emancipated in the South than in the North, and freedmen in the South were incomparably better off than freedmen in the North.[28]

The law governing the emancipation of slaves can be traced to *Sommersett's Case,* 20 Howell's St. Tr. 1 at 80-82 (K. B. 1771), wherein Lord Mansfield held that slavery was contrary to natural law, therefore not protected by the common law, and sustainable only under a positive act of Parliament, and that, therefore, when a slave was brought by his master to England untouched by any statute allowing such bondage, the slave became forever free. Transportation by the master onto free soil meant freedom to a slave.

Mansfield's judgment was in turn based on earlier judgments of the King's Bench. From and after the Norman Conquest, the feudal system became entrenched in England, and part of this social and legal structure was the institution of villeinage under which white Anglo-Saxon people of the realm were for hundreds of years held in bondage not materially different from the bondage of the black African race in North America. Villeinage was phased out by the judges of the common law, faithful to the demand in the 29th article of the Magna Carta of King Henry III: "Nullus liber homo disseisietur de liberis consuetudinibus suis," —No freeman shall be denied the benefit of customs which make him free.

By ancient custom, every statute, rule, and plea was construed and applied, whenever possible, in favor of liberating a man from bondage and making him free. If a lord conveyed a freehold to his villein, the grantee automatically became a freeman. If a villein sued his lord in a court of common law, and the lord answered to the merits without first interposing a plea to disability on account of bondage, the villein automatically became a freeman. And so it went. In the case of *Pigg v. Caley,* Noy 27 (K. B. 1618), villeinage felt the frowns of the common law for the last time, and disappeared in history without an emancipation proclamation, civil war, or constitutional amendment.

When Thomas Jefferson penned language first appearing in the Northwest Ordinance of 1787, and later used in the Missouri Compromise and 13th Amendment, he wrote that "neither slavery nor involuntary servitude" should be lawful, because he meant to prohibit villeinage as well as slavery, and to spare whites as well as blacks from any capitalization of labor on any pretext ancient or modern.

In any event, the circuit court of Missouri granted Scott and his family their freedom as a matter of course on established law and rudimentary principle. A Southern judge, in a Southern court, on

Southern jurisprudence, freed these slaves effortlessly and quickly.

It is hard to understand why Irene Emerson took an appeal. The facts were clear. The law was settled against her. The appeal was certain to be expensive and time-consuming. Assuming honest administration of justice, it was obvious that she could not prevail. Mrs. Emerson was getting on in years, and she was too old to weather the experience. Especially after the judgment of the circuit court, which was a cloud on the master's title, the fair market value of Scott and his family as slaves was probably less than the cost of taking the cause up to the Missouri Supreme Court. The wager was plainly not worth the risk.

Dred Scott was a poor black with no resources to speak of. He was evidently represented before the circuit court by a lawyer doing him an act of kindness, a member of the bar doing his ethical duty to render some services to the needy at reduced or no fees, especially where rights were manifest and in need of vindication. Irene Emerson was not wealthy, neither was John Sandford, her eventual successor in title. The parties in this litigation were ordinary folks, unable to afford major litigation.

The case was of a kind which, if pushed, would have to aim at reversing judicial trends going back hundreds of years. It was the kind of case that could consume prime years in the careers of high-powered and expensive lawyers, and such lawyers started to come aboard for Mrs. Emerson after the initial routine encounter before the circuit court of Missouri. As things turned out, the cause was pending before one tribunal or another over eleven strenuous years.

The history of the case after the judgment of the circuit court of Missouri is exceedingly long and tortured. A routine affair hardly worth notice was dilated by straining the legal system into a production as inflammatory as *Uncle Tom's Cabin*. The case was obviously bankrolled by wealthy interests—on both sides by the time the case found its way into Federal courts—, for there is no other plausible way to explain what happened. The investors in this cause must have aimed at exciting passions violent enough to ignite a civil war. Certainly, nobody pouring funds into the affair cared about Dred Scott. Had philanthropy been the concern, the freedom of Scott and his family could have been quickly purchased for much less than what it cost to mount subsequent rounds of this stupendous litigation. It is impossible to believe that those funding this very expensive venture did not understand the political dynamite involved and the fuse they were lighting. And their barratry achieved the kind of mischief which they must have foreseen.

Mysteriously, two of the three members of the Missouri Supreme Court wholly disregarded a massive corpus of Southern jurisprudence, which they did not even cite, then held that Scott and his family were still slaves, thus reversing the circuit court which had liberated them.

Yet as appears in *Dred Scott v. Emerson,* 15 Mo. 576 at 587-592 (1852), Chief Justice Hamilton Gamble wrote a learned dissent, copiously laying down the law as given by the Emperor Justinian and Lord Coke up to the very recent past. He protested, "In this State, it has been recognized, from the beginning of the government, as a correct position in law, that a master who takes his slave to reside in a State or territory where slavery is prohibited, thereby emancipates his slave." He then cited and expounded no less than eight reported decisions of the Missouri Supreme Court, all cited by Scott's counsel and directly on point. He expounded the first case, *Winney v. Whitesides,* 1 Mo. 473 (1824), then observed, "The principle thus settled runs through all the cases subsequently decided, for they were all cases in which the right to freedom was claimed in our courts, under a residence in a free State or territory, and where there had been no adjudication upon the right to freedom in such State or territory." He added that the Missouri Supreme Court, "so far from standing alone on this question, is supported by the decisions of other slave States, including those in which it may be supposed there was the least disposition in favor of emancipation." Thereupon, he discussed reported decisions in Louisiana, Mississippi, Virginia, and Kentucky, all concurring with the reported decisions in Missouri which unequivocally demanded the freedom of Scott and his family.

Even counsel for Mrs. Emerson conceded all the decisions of the Missouri Supreme Court under which Scott and his family were entitled to their freedom. As if it were an argument for slavery, counsel lamented one Mr. Justice Thompkins, who "was a great apostle of freedom," and thought "the evil should be restricted as much as possible." The same observation could have been made concerning the judges of the King's Bench who had ordained, on the basis of Magna Carta, that villeins and slaves should be deemed free whenever any fair legal reason could be advanced in their behalf.

A majority of the Missouri Supreme Court were not confused, and had not overlooked the unambiguous precedents which established the applicable law. All questions of property in slaves and conflict of laws had been definitively settled, nor was there any honest way to distinguish or overrule the precedents before them. The problem was not prejudice or ignorance, because a trained lawyer or judge knows how to read a dozen or more cases all going the same way and apply them to facts admitted on the record. There is only one plausible explanation for the misconduct of the two appellate judges who ruled against Scott and his family. Raw corruption, induced by bribery or otherwise, was nothing new in their day, and has not since ceased to trouble mankind. This perennial flaw in temporal justice is condemned in holy scripture, and over passing centuries judges have been impeached and even hanged for it, yet never has the problem been eradicated.

By a winding and fantastic path which defied res judicata and other basic principles, the case of Dred Scott was recommenced before a circuit court of the United States, and finally reached the highest court of the land on writ of error, and there it was twice argued. It was decided in *Dred Scott v. Sandford,* 19 Howard 393 (U.S. 1857), on a vote of 7-2, that Scott and his family were, after all, slaves. And they were slaves, said the majority incredibly, because the Missouri Compromise was unconstitutional. The Missouri Compromise was simply an extension of the Northwest Ordinance, as reenacted by Congress in 1789 in exercise of undoubted constitutional powers, to territory west of the Mississippi River. In his "opinion of the court," Chief Justice Roger B. Taney ignored the judgment of Lord Mansfield in 1771, and the decisions of high courts across the Southern States following Lord Mansfield's judgment. Chief Justice Taney was fully aware of the judgments of the King's Bench, the cases given reference by Judge Gamble of Missouri, and a good many other like cases reported from judicial records in the Dixie States, yet he did not even mention them.

Oddly enough, Taney was one of the greatest lawyers of his age. As attorney general of the United States, he had written the message of President Andrew Jackson accompanying the veto of the bill to extend the charter of the Second Bank of the United States.[29] His last formal opinion in *Ex Parte Merryman,* 17 Fed. Cas. 144 (U.S. Cir. Ct. Md. 1861), forbidding Presidential suspension of the writ of habeas corpus, was one of the most courageous and magnificent judicial acts in American history.

It seems difficult to imagine how such an extraordinary man could be corrupted. But Sir Francis Bacon, as Lord Chancellor of England, was impeached and convicted of bribery, and, if such a great philosopher could be corrupted, so too could Chief Justice Taney. And a judge can be led astray by inducements subtler than cash in envelopes or promises of favor. Even a great man on the bench can be secretly and privately flattered, cajoled, or duped into doing what is expected of him, or his political passions can be inspired into rendering a dubious judgment, without an actual offer of consideration.[30]

In genteel circumstances rich, powerful, and influential men could have made known their wishes to Taney in refined language, accompanied by deference to his high station. It could have been done so smoothly that the stink of corruption might not have been apparent even to some of those participating. In this way cases have been "fixed" to suit ends other than justice.[31]

An indignant admirer of Taney might protest that surely this great Chief Justice was not bribed. And the answer to such a protest must be that Taney was probably not bribed. He had all the money he needed, and he was too old for other allurements. But the case surely was discussed by great men in his presence, suggestions must have been dropped, and he must have understood what was desired by men whom he respected on account of their wealth or standing. For there can be no doubt that rich, powerful, and influential men in the United States thought it would be a good thing to get rid of the Missouri Compromise, not only by legislative repeal but also by judicial holding. And it is now known and no longer concealed that, during the deliberations of the court on the fate of Dred Scott and his family, at least two members of the court were actively lobbied by President-Elect James Buchanan. It is no longer the well-kept secret it once was that the President-Elect communicated first with Justice John Catron, and then urged Justice Robert Grier to be sensible in joining with others on the court in finding the Missouri Compromise unconstitutional.[32] Others on the court must also have been told what was expected on them. In any event, Taney, Catron, Grier, and others on the court did exactly what such rich, powerful, and influential men wanted them to do.

The anticlimax was that, after they had been used like pieces of furniture on the legal stage for more than a decade, and found to be slaves, Scott and his family were all freed by their master Sandford.[33] It is, therefore, obvious that the soul of the case had been collusion for dark ulterior motives.

The effect of the judgment was outrage across the North, including accusations of corruption, which were surely not far from the truth, and hatred of the South for enslaving Dred Scott, which rather missed the mark, for the South had actually freed Scott, his wife, and his daughters. The situation was by then agitated to the point at which people from the two sections could joyfully kill each other, —perfect for the civil war soon to begin. It is impossible to believe that those who created this situation with their boundless resources did not foresee and desire the trouble they had produced by persistent effort over some years.

The Democratic National Convention of 1860 in Charleston

The next chapter in this continuing saga was John Brown's raid, which we now definitively know was produced by a conspiracy of wealthy men behind the scenes and likewise was drummed up into a tornado of hatred between the North and the South. Then came the Presidential election of 1860.

The Democratic Party was a coalition of conservative voices in the North and the South. Because they were a coalition with broad support throughout the country, they had controlled the White House twenty-four of thirty-two years since the election of Andrew Jackson. The Whigs had been their main competition, but were in decline. The Republicans were emerging from the repeal of the Missouri Compromise, but had strength only in the North. The Democrats needed only to stick together, and, if they had done so, they would have prevailed again in 1860. As it was, the Democrats split in two, with "Union" Democrats in the North, "National" Democrats for the South, and the old Whigs running as the "Constitutional Union" Party. The result was so predictable that Abraham Lincoln simply sat at home in Illinois and awaited his inevitable election without giving a single campaign speech. It is a mistake to view the situation merely by counting popular and electoral votes as cast in the Presidential election of that year.[34] If there had not been two Democratic candidates for President, the conservatives could have challenged the Republicans instead of each other, and their united voice of moderation would easily have carried the whole South, all the border States, and key States in the North. Even as it was, the two Democratic candidates, with division between them, easily carried the popular vote against Lincoln by a large margin, and united they would have considerably enhanced it, thereby bringing in the electoral votes needed to carry the Presidency.

The question is why there were two Democratic tickets. Superficially considered, it appears that the factious behavior of eight Southern delegations at the Democratic National Convention of 1860 in Charleston was responsible for the split, which was followed by further splintering by Southerners in Baltimore.

Stephen Douglas was the leading Democrat running for President, but he was ardently opposed by Southern delegates, because his wheeling and dealing for the Kansas-Nebraska Act had given their region worthless concessions in a minor part of the Louisiana Purchase in exchange for a transcontinental railroad between Chicago and San Francisco.

True it is that the cheated Southerners should have listened to Sam Houston. They should never have given up on their demands for a transcontinental railroad between New Orleans and San Diego for a worthless opportunity to make Kansas a slave State.

Southern legislators had been short-sighted, and had helped to upset a solemn agreement embodied in the Missouri Compromise on which the stability of the Union depended. And so if the political deal behind the Kansas-Nebraska Act had been a formal contract all legal and proper, a suit brought by them in equity to rescind it would have been barred by unclean hands.

But the political deal behind the Missouri Compromise was not a formal contract all legal and proper. It was an understanding among politicians, resting on mutual trust. And it was, after all, a swindle. Never mind that those swindled had not themselves been innocent victims. Douglas, the swindler, had been found out, and so could not thereafter claim to be a gentleman in the eyes of those whom he had wronged.

Southern delegations at the convention in Charleston prevented the nomination of Douglas over fifty-seven ballots. And they walked out over failure of a resolution denying the power of territorial legislatures to prohibit slavery. The resolution was wrong in principle, because it contradicted Lord Mansfield. And the resolution was utterly meaningless, because, especially with the pending entry of Kansas into the Union as a free State, the Federal territories could nowhere accommodate slavery even if nowhere prohibited by law. By this gesture of theatrical indignation, the Southern delegates walking out of the Democratic convention in Charleston guaranteed the election of Lincoln as President.

If those Southern delegations had stayed in Charleston, if they had displayed discipline and shrewdness as patriots, they could have secured the nomination of John Breckenridge of Kentucky for Vice President as a running mate with Stephen Douglas for President. Had Breckenridge been on the ticket with Douglas, the Democrats would have been unbeatable. Breckenridge was already the youngest man ever to have been Vice President, then serving under the incumbent President James

Buchanan. Breckenridge was a statesman of the very highest order, universally respected.[35] The United States suffered because political fate never allowed Breckenridge to rise to the fullness of his enormous potential.

If Breckenridge had been elected with Douglas, there would have been no withdrawal of Southern States from the Union. And Breckenridge would have become President when Douglas unexpectedly died in June 1861. He would have been the greatest President of his century. He would have wisely guided the country to build transcontinental railroads for the South as well as the North, and to nudge slavery into extinction in a manner mutually beneficial to the white race and the black race.

There is no way to excuse the short-sightedness of those Southern delegations in Charleston. They proved only that the heat of political passion is dangerous, especially in unsettled times.

But more is required than identifying the shortcomings of politicians, as may be illustrated. Philippe, Duc d'Orléans, in betraying his kinsman Louis XVI, succumbed to temptation: hoping to become King himself, he used his immense fortune to help foment the French Revolution. He deserves no sympathy for his personal fate. But France did not deserve the horrors of upheaval and chaos which he and others visited upon her. Nor should Orléans have been tempted to indulge in such folly. The true wrongdoers were the conspirators who seduced him for their wicked purposes.

And likewise, the Southern delegations in Charleston should never have allowed themselves to be provoked into the heat of political passion. Douglas should never have swindled Southern legislators to get their assistance in repealing the Missouri Compromise. And railroad magnates and great financiers should not have cynically misused their power in buying Douglas. With these conspirators the ultimate responsibility lies for the calamity of the Democratic convention at Charleston in the spring of 1860. The United States had the right to enjoy an honest election, unpolluted by mischief behind the scenes.

The Question of Protective Tariffs

Like those financing John Brown's raid, the plotters behind the mass marketing of *Uncle Tom's Cabin,* the repeal of the Missouri Compromise, the civil war in the Kansas Territory, the corrupt influence in the case of Dred Scott, the splitting of the Democrats in Charleston, and other such events up through Fort Sumter, were respectable men of wealth, —men with more financial power than they could wield for their own good and the good of mankind. It is true as Lord Acton said that "historic responsibility has to make up for the want of legal responsibility."[36] But in assessing responsibility for the sake of history, it is important not to convict the wrong culprits.

Abraham Lincoln and others in his party were wrong in blaming Southern planters. And yet it is a mistake to blame Lincoln for his views expressed with characteristic frankness when he said, "My politics are short and sweet, like the old woman's dance. I am in favor of a national bank, the internal improvements system, and a high protective tariff."[37] Lincoln cannot be condemned for embracing ideas also favored by such exalted American patriots as Alexander Hamilton and Henry Clay. No less a Jeffersonian democrat than John Calhoun understood the need for a national bank[38] and a protective tariff.[39] Of all things, transcontinental railroads were internal improvements, and in 1860 both wings of the Democratic Party, no less than the Republicans, favored the aid of the Federal government to build transcontinental railroads.[40] The problem, therefore, was neither a national bank, nor internal improvements, nor protective tariffs, nor an agenda including them.

It has been respectably proposed that the American Civil War was caused by abusive imposition of protective tariffs.[41] The theme has often been heard over many years that Northern industrialists wanted to tax the Southern States into poverty, and to use all or most the money for internal improvements above the Mason-Dixon Line and the Ohio River. And this claimed exploitation is supposed to explain why the Southern States seceded from the Union, and why Northern industrialists prompted Lincoln to start a war of conquest against the Old South.

It is true that protective tariffs had been a problem during the antebellum period. The question came to a head during the South Carolina nullification crisis in 1832 and 1833,[42] but thereafter was fairly resolved as the bare facts show.

Tariffs are duties on imports routinely imposed by the nations of the earth both for the raising of revenue and the regulation of trade. During the antebellum period, tariffs were the principal means of raising revenue for the government of the United States. Shortly after the inauguration of George Washington, Congress laid tariffs to raise revenue adequate for running the Federal government, and also to provide moderate protection of some American industries from foreign competition.[43] Ad valorem rates, depending on article, ran from 5 to 12½%. No significant protest was heard against this regime or its purposes.

After the War of 1812, various protective tariffs, above revenue levels and for regulatory purposes, were imposed during the presidencies of James Madison and James Monroe.[44] Ad valorem rates, depending on article, advanced to the range of 15 to 30%, and these duties were generally acceptable.

The trouble began with the so-called tariff of abominations,[45] enacted not so much to raise revenues or to protect industries as to engineer the election of Andrew Jackson as President. The original plan was to set rates so high that the incumbent John Quincy Adams would veto the bill, then to blame Adams for failing to protect industries in the mid-Atlantic States whose electoral votes Jackson sought. To the surprise of all, Adams signed the bill. John Randolph of Roanoke poignantly asserted that the "bill referred to manufactures of no sort or kind, but the manufacture of a President of the United States." Still benefiting from his image as the "hero of New Orleans," Jackson was elected anyway. Under this illicit manipulation of the power to tax imports, duties were raised as high as 50% ad valorem on an expanded list of dutiable items.

The legislation triggered a recession in the Southern States. The problem became serious, but was addressed successfully by constitutional processes which saved the Union. The people of South Carolina met in convention, declared the tariff of abominations unconstitutional, and threatened secession from the Union. President Jackson issued a proclamation denouncing the resistance as treason and threatening civil war. The legislature of the State passed resolutions defying Federal authority and prepared military forces to meet invasion. Daniel Webster and John Calhoun faced each other in a memorable oratorical encounter in the United States Senate, while Henry Clay engineered a compromise tariff,[46] which expanded the list of duty-free goods and gradually reduced duties over the next decade to revenue levels, by that time, about 20% ad valorem on an agreed list, whereupon the crisis passed, and the Union waxed strong again.

Thereafter, a new protective tariff was attempted,[47] but was soon trimmed,[48] and the program was eliminated in 1857 on the day before James Buchanan became President.[49] An enlarged duty-free list was established, and a tariff of 20% ad valorem was imposed on selected items, yielding revenues sufficient only to pay the expenses of the Federal government.

In 1860, therefore, there was no protective tariff at all, only a moderate revenue tariff. If more internal improvements had been built in the Northern States during the antebellum period, the Southern States undertook most of the export business, which they carried on tax-free, because export duties were constitutionally prohibited,[50] and income taxes at uniform rates were not then constitutionally authorized.[51] While shipbuilding and shipping were done mainly by interests in the Northern States, there were no navigation acts prohibiting shipbuilding or shipping by interests in the Southern States. In general, the Old South benefited greatly from the growing self-sufficiency of the interacting network of States within the Union, as had been envisioned by John Calhoun after the War of 1812, including protection of their vast international trade provided by the navy of the United States.[52]

Complaints about unjust tariffs had been a venerable tradition in Southern politics during the antebellum period, nor had the subject worn out as a favorite theme of harangues in the Dixie States even after Buchanan's inauguration. Yet by 1860 there were no longer any objective facts to give thunder to the speeches. Secession was not an economic necessity for the Southern States. On the contrary, the Union was for them an economic blessing.

The election of a Republican as President did not automatically translate into injurious tariffs. Only after Southern States seceded from the Union was it possible, beginning in the spring of 1861 and in successive stages thereafter, to enact a regime of protective tariffs throughout the rest of the century.[53] Alexander Stephens was the wisest statesman of the Old South. While nobody has ever given a finer defense of secession as a right under the intended meaning of the United States Constitution,[54] Stephens demonstrated in his "Union" speech before the legislature of Georgia following Lincoln's election[55] that, if the Southern States had remained in the Union, they would have been able to weather the Republican victory. If the South was heavily outnumbered in the House, she had easily enough members in the Senate to unite with moderates in the North and in this way to block exploitive imposition of protective tariffs.

Viewed dispassionately, unjust tariffs were a potential irritant, but they created no pressure contributing significantly to the breakup of the Union in 1860-1861 and the American Civil War. The real stakes in political events then unfolding were far more important.

Banking and Currency and the Money Trust

Large banking houses in the United States and Europe were the culprits who paid for Mrs. Stowe's vicious pen, bought the repeal of the

Missouri Compromise, stirred up trouble in the Kansas Territory, corrupted the judicial process in the case of Dred Scott, and laid the foundations for the breakup of the Democratic convention in Charleston. They have since escaped the censure of historians, as they have hid behind a smoke screen of freeing the slaves and saving the Union.

In order to understand the machinations of these financiers, it will be necessary to become acquainted with Charles A. Lindbergh Sr., father of the famous aviator, who represented the 6th district of Minnesota in Congress from 1907 to 1917. Congressman Lindbergh transcended partisan politics by the uniqueness of his insights and contributions. After serving as an "insurgent" Republican in Congress, Lindbergh became one of the founding fathers of the Farmer-Labor Party, which later merged with the Democratic establishment in what became known as the Minnesota DFL. He ran for governor in the Republican primary of Minnesota in 1918, endorsed by the Non-Partisan League. As he began his campaign, he was smeared by several large newspapers in New York City controlled by major financial interests on Wall Street. For he was no ordinary politician running for public office in the Upper Mississippi Valley. During his campaign he was hung in effigy and branded as "disloyal," a "traitor," and a "free love Bolshevik." His campaign car was shot at in Rock County. And, nine days before the primary vote, he was arrested in Martin County on trumped-up charges which were conveniently dropped after he placed second in the four-way primary on a strong showing of 41%.

Why was Lindbergh so feared by the great banking houses on Wall Street? He was feared because he knew his critics better than they would have preferred. He published the truth about the sordid origins of their financial empire in his classic polemic against the Federal Reserve Act of 1913, entitled *Banking and Currency and the Money Trust,* National Capital Press, Washington, 1913, particularly pages 83-107.

Lindbergh struggled without much success to construct a cogent theory of paper money, which was really rather beside the point.

From an historical point of view, for those interested, it is plain enough that the Philadelphia Convention understood the power of Congress to coin money as nothing other than the power to strike gold and silver into defined pieces of legal tender.[56] The framers were not sentimentalists seeking to impose archaic principles on the nature of money. They understood that money does not have to be made of gold or silver to function as money. But out of a desire to limit deficit spending, to restrain inflation of paper currency, and generally to circumscribe the power of the Federal government, they resorted to the time-honored expedient of gold and silver coin minted by public authority as the only legal tender. For if currency and credit are redeemable in gold and silver coin as the only legal tender, the amount of currency in circulation and credit outstanding cannot exceed the amount required for current transactions, plus the amount of specie on deposit. And, if only gold and silver coin may be legal tender, government cannot spend more than public revenues received, plus whatever will voluntarily be accepted in its notes, bonds, and credit. Conceivably the framers might have attempted another remedy, but they adopted gold and silver coin as the constitutional standard. Solid legal scholarship is available on this point. As good a source as any is found in the dissenting opinion of Justice Samuel Field in *Juilliard v. Greenman,* 110 U.S. 421 at 451-470 (1884). The use of paper currency, circulating by fiat as legal tender, was only one of many innovations which arose from the ashes to which the United States Constitution had been reduced by the American Civil War.

Lindbergh's effort to justify a system of paper money was also beside the point, because money is more than a medium of exchange. Economists have fairly debated which medium is best. Gold, silver, and paper disciplined one way or another each have certain advantages and disadvantages, nor need that question be settled here. For the really important question in every case should be, Who controls the gold, the silver, or the paper? Whoever has this control can expand or contract currency and credit, can direct or redirect the flow of whatever passes as money, and thereby can stimulate or enfeeble any activity which requires money or its practical equivalent. Compared to the power of increasing and diminishing the money supply, the powers of commanding armies and fleets, making or executing laws, or taxing one thing or another are less important, for none of these activities can occur without money.

The power to create and annul money should never become a private franchise. Sir William Blackstone thus expressed the idea: "The coining of money is in all states an act of the sovereign power."[57] So things were at one time, and so things should be today. Money should always be created or annulled by public authority, which alone can be so identified, regulated, limited, counterbalanced, supervised, and audited that it can safely be entrusted with such an immense prerogative, and the responsibility to exercise it impartially for the general good of society. Unfortunately, the power to create and annul money can be and has been subverted from time to time in history by private interests up to no good. It is a sad tale how this public authority was subverted by private interests in the United States, and this sad tale was capably told by Congressman Lindbergh.

His most valuable insights are found in his tracing of events which began with the American Civil War after it had been provoked by orchestrated events during the 1850s. In his book, and again in a resolution he introduced in Congress, Lindbergh quoted and commented upon an infamous solicitation known as the "Hazard Circular," which, never having been of public record, was saved by private individuals approached, and by them was then made known. Icy silence and mystery surround it. The best authentication of this extraordinary document, aside from the authority of Lindbergh, is that it so well explains legislation passed by Congress on banking and currency during and after the American Civil War.

The circular, as far as can be descried, was distributed by Jay Cooke & Co. of Philadelphia, representing financiers then associated with Junius Morgan, who in 1854 had become a partner in the banking firm of Peabody, Morgan & Co. in London, to which he succeeded in 1864 as J. S. Morgan & Co. The House of Morgan had affiliates in New York, beginning with Duncan, Sherman & Co. in 1857, then Dabney, Morgan & Co. in 1864, then Drexel, Morgan & Co. in 1871, and eventually J. P. Morgan & Co in 1895, not to mention affiliates on the continent of Europe. The same circular was probably also distributed by August Belmont & Co. of New York, representing financiers then associated with James Rothschild in Paris, including N. M. Rothschild & Co. in London which largely controlled the Bank of England. The House of Rothschild was also affiliated with certain firms on the continent of Europe. Morgan and Rothschild were allied and mighty names in high finance then, and their successors in interest have the same awesome power today.

The Hazard Circular was, in any event, distributed among wealthy citizens in the Northern States in 1862, seeking their investment in war bonds to pay for the military conquest of the Southern States. It contains the following language:

> "Slavery is likely to be abolished by the war power, and all chattel slavery abolished. This I and my friends are in favor of, for slavery is but the owning of labor and carries with it the care of the laborers, while the European plan, led on by England, is that capital shall control labor by controlling wages. The great debt that capitalists will see to it is made out of the war must be used as a means to control the volume of money. To accomplish this, the bonds must be used as a banking basis. We are now waiting for the secretary of the treasury to make this recommendation to

Congress. It will not do to allow the greenback, as it is called, to circulate as money any length of time, as we cannot control that. But we can control the bonds and through the bonds the bank issues. "

The financiers' motives in the war were not as glorious as the motives of many fine young men when they marched in ranks mowed down at Second Manassas, Fredericksburg, the Wilderness, Spotsylvania, Second Cold Harbor, and other such battles. The true object, for which those boys were uncaringly and needlessly sacrificed, was to transform national debt into private control of banking and currency in the United States.

Greenbacks mentioned in this circular, properly called United States notes, were paper currency issued by Congress to pay for the war, consisting of interest-free promises to pay dollars at such time in the future as Congress should elect, meanwhile ordained legal tender for most debts public and private.[58] The expedient was used for a while in the Northern States, but it eventually ceased to be effective as the war assumed gigantic proportions that most people never dreamed of. The great banking houses in Philadelphia, New York, London, and Paris did not like this currency, because they could not "control" it, —in other words, they could not convert it into a profitable venture for themselves. So they hoped to displace such fiat currency with a "sound" currency based on war bonds, which they and their choice customers came to hold in large quantities.

The war bonds were more than interest-bearing instruments, because they could be and were transformed into a privileged system of banking and currency under the National Bank Act of 1864.[59] A new system of national banks was capitalized in part by gold and silver coin and greenbacks, but one-third or more of the stock had to be purchased with war bonds. These bonds were then received by the treasury department as security for national bank notes. These national bank notes, even if receivable in payment of Federal taxes but not generally legal tender, were the practical equivalent of cash because they were backed by bonds, and could be used to mount loans at interest to private borrowers and as fractional reserves for private deposits. And interest on the bonds was meanwhile paid in specie to national banks whose owners, therefore, earned double interest. Meanwhile, the currency of banks chartered by the several States was taxed out of circulation,[60] requiring them to do business in specie, greenbacks, and national bank notes and to maintain deposits with national banks as reserves. When, therefore, Jay Cooke and August Belmont sold war bonds under seemingly respectable auspices, they sold an exceedingly valuable franchise to private interests, when that franchise should have remained with public authority. Their best customers were not patriots rallying around the flag, but self-seeking adventurers buying, at bargain prices, the monetary independence of the United States.

A new regime of taxation, including not only higher tariffs but income taxes,[61] was enacted to sustain this enterprise profitable to the large banking houses, which alone had sufficient resources and bonds for capitalization of national banks. These institutions included central reserve banks on Wall Street, which insured and nourished the whole system of institutions growing up from financing the American Civil War.

The cunning sophistication that planned, incited, and financed the brutal conquest of the Southern States was utterly beyond the comprehension of most people then living in the region. For their civilization was quiet, tradition-minded, agrarian, and quasi-feudal. Their tastes were simple, but classical and refined, as reflected in their architecture, monuments, and landscapes. By temperament, they were sober, plain, and religious, even tending toward the mystical. Their view of life was imbued with a sense of chivalry. They believed that the war would be fought on the field of honor in a few battles which they would win, as at First Manassas, whereupon public opinion and civilized values would concede their independence. But such a war was not what had been engineered by high finance, and the Southern people were wholly unprepared to resist the juggernaut which had been ruthlessly bought to march against them.

And in appreciating this reality, the writing of J. B. Jones is particularly helpful. Born in Maryland, Jones spent his youth in Kentucky and Missouri, then married into the Custis family on Virginia's eastern shore. He had a successful antebellum career as a novelist and newspaper editor in Baltimore. After 1857 he edited a periodical published from offices in Philadelphia, and from there he was able to observe trends in Northern politics and business. When the war came, he moved with his family to Richmond to be with his people in time of crisis. He was too old to fight on the field, so he offered his services to the Confederate government and was engaged as a clerk in the war department. During the four ensuing years, Jones wrote his day-by-day account, published as *A Rebel War Clerk's Diary* only months after his death in early 1866 by J. B. Lippincott & Co. of Philadelphia.

Jones's entries shortly before and after Fort Sumter[62] relate his conversations with prominent Southern leaders, including Henry Wise who had

been Governor of Virginia and later served throughout the war as a
Confederate brigadier general on the York Peninsula. Jones noted that
capitalists on Wall Street were anxious to finance the war. Their objectives, as Lindbergh later noted, included a market of cheap black labor
for them to hire at low wages, as well as confiscation of Southern lands
to pay the expenses of conquest. Drawing from his observations in the
North, Jones warned Governor Wise that the 70,000 militia called up by
Lincoln in the spring of 1861 were only vedettes of a planned army of
700,000 which would invade on the false pretext of saving the Union and
freeing the slaves, but for the real purpose of confiscating Southern
wealth. Wise reacted to these predictions in astonished disbelief, unable
to comprehend that anybody then living would dare undertake such a
monstrous crime before the witness of an enlightened world.

In contrast to the monetary apparatus of the North, Confederate
finance was pathetic and lamentable.[63] The Confederate government was
able to raise some specie by the sale of bonds early in the war, but this
amount was hardly enough to fund any significant proportion of treasury
notes issuing from Richmond as the principal means to pay for the war.
Heavy taxation required to fund those notes was not feasible, and only
the sale of bonds served to soak up excess currency. But the bonds were
hardly sufficient for this purpose, for people generally preferred to
invest their redundant notes in tangibles, causing prices to skyrocket
and speculation to run rampant. Burdened with a notoriously weak
currency and runaway inflation, the South was no match for the North.

Early in the war there was an opportunity to issue Confederate bonds
for the purchase of cotton from Southern plantations at a price of 10¢ a
pound, and then, before the Union blockade became too strong, to ship
the cotton incrementally over the course of a year to Europe where it
could have earned credits in powerful specie-paying institutions, based on
market prices of cotton in England and France at 20-30, and even 50¢ a
pound. The conditions of war created such an artificial disparity in the
price of cotton on either side of the Atlantic. Under the circumstances
Southern planters had practically no other buyer than the Confederate
government, and European manufacturers groaned from a shortage of
cotton. Up to four million bales might conceivably have been transported
to Europe during the first year of the war, before the blockade became too
strong. Even a meaningful fraction of the whole crop, say half or even a
quarter or less, if transported in a timely manner, might have provided
credits so substantial that the Confederate States could have purchased

ironclad steamers in Europe, used those warships to break the blockade and keep commerce open, and sustained the value of their treasury notes. With a stronger currency, the South could have fed, clothed, and equipped her armies properly, and would have had a much better opportunity to win independence. The idea was rejected, because President Davis and his circle in Richmond believed that an embargo upon cotton would promote speedy recognition of the Confederate States by the nations of Europe, and that the Union blockade would be ineffective and last no more than a year.

In going into the war, the Southern people did not know the Union would be hijacked and mortgaged so completely that the United States Constitution, as the framers had known it, would cease to exist. They rested their case on constitutional principles which were abolished by force of arms financed by moneylenders. During the course of the war, they learned this ugly truth from the acrimonious experience of blood, tears, tragedy, and ruin. In this light, it is understandable that cultivated Southerners thought of Yankee mentality as barbarism, which in truth it was, yet in failing to make wise use of resources the Confederate government undercut necessary defense against the onslaught.

The fantastic power grab by great financiers did not end with the war, but continued in grand style thereafter. And in this connection, it is worthwhile to pay some attention to the little noticed fourth section of the 14th Amendment, which says, "The validity of the public debt of the United States, authorized by law, including debts incurred for the payment of pensions and bounties for services in suppressing insurrection or rebellion, shall not be questioned."

In those days, it was forcefully argued by Henry Clay Dean and other peace Democrats that the national debt incurred in waging the war against the Southern States was unjust and unconstitutional, that it was a breach of public trust, that it should be repudiated outright, and that it could not be imposed on future generations.[64] The real purpose of the fourth section of the 14th Amendment, stripped of its appeal to the gallery on taking care of old soldiers, was to silence characters like Dean, and to institutionalize the national debt which had been monetized through the National Bank Act of 1864, thereby making permanent the grip which Morgan, Rothschild, and their affiliates had acquired upon banking and currency in the United States.

It is particularly ironic that this so-called constitutional amendment was unconstitutionally imposed upon the country.[65] A full discussion of why the 14th Amendment was not lawfully adopted can become protracted. But the explanation cutting to the quick is that ratifications by ten Southern States were unconstitutionally coerced by the first Reconstruction Act.[66] For the Act abolished free governments and suspended the writ of habeas corpus in ten of the conquered Southern States, placing them all under martial law in time of profound peace, and in such condition they were to remain unless and until they adopted the 14th Amendment. But the United States Supreme Court had already held that Congress had no constitutional authority to impose martial law except in the actual theater of invasion or rebellion.[67] If Congress can under some circumstances impose martial law to make war,[68] it certainly cannot under any circumstances impose martial law to force adoption of a constitutional amendment. Since martial law imposed by the first Reconstruction Act was obviously unconstitutional, the ratifications thereby coerced had no lawful force and effect. And without the voluntary ratifications of those ten States, the 14th Amendment could not have been, and so never was lawfully adopted.

The great usurpations of high finance after the war were explained with precision by Alexander Del Mar, an engineer who served on the United States Monetary Commission of 1876. Del Mar was originally appointed because he knew how to extract precious metals from the earth. Yet he soon grasped the real problem, which was that per capita the supply of money across the country was steadily decreasing, thereby steadily enhancing the value of the national debt held by the financial empire of Morgan, Rothschild, and their affiliates. The engineer undertook a deep study in which he discovered an important causal relationship, evident over long ages, between an optimum money supply and the general state of civilization. He was not too preoccupied with the question whether money should be gold, silver, or paper. For him, it was mainly the law making an item legal tender that created money and gave it value. In his mind, the question was always how best to exploit historical and political circumstances to achieve an optimum quantity and flow of money.

Del Mar's understanding deepened as he examined the origins of the East India Company and the Bank of England in the 17th Century, for these particulars enabled him to see clearly that the power to coin money is a power for which men have long conspired, often using foul methods, and that such plotting and scheming have frequently had important impact in shaping human events for the worse. Beginning as a competent engineer, he became a remarkable historian, then matured into a distinguished and respected economist. Applying the wisdom which his endeavors had taught him, Del Mar provided an intriguing and instructive account of the Presidential election of 1868.[69]

A very large quantity of war bonds had, of course, been purchased by the syndicate of financiers headed by Junius Morgan and James Rothschild. The bonds in question had been authorized by Congress,[70] but the statutory language did not clearly say whether repayment of principal should be in gold or greenbacks. It so happens that August Belmont, agent for the House of Rothschild, had become the national chairman and political boss of the Democratic Party in the United States. And he was the secret owner of *The New York World,* a very powerful newspaper and the primary mouthpiece of the Democratic Party, although Belmont's control of the newspaper was not widely understood at the time. At the Democratic National Convention in 1868, the delegates led by the likes of Henry Clay Dean voted a platform plank which said that war bonds should be repaid in greenbacks, save where gold was expressly mentioned in the statute authorizing the securities. Belmont naturally understood that the financial interests he represented would not be pleased.

George Pendleton, it so happened, agreed with the platform pledge to pay off war bonds with greenbacks, and was winning votes at the convention for nomination as President, yet suddenly he withdrew for no apparent reason, stepping aside in favor of Horatio Seymour who was thought to favor repayment of war bonds in gold. However, to the surprise of the financiers in Europe, Seymour acquiesced to the platform plank and called for repayment in greenbacks. The political fortunes of the Democrats began to rise, and it appeared that Seymour would be elected President. Yet, suddenly, only three weeks before the election, *The New York World* published an editorial saying that Seymour could not win, and that somebody else ought to be nominated in his place. In the resulting confusion, the Republican candidate General Ulysses S. Grant won the election by an unconvincing margin in the popular vote, and he assured repayment of the bonds in gold.

Belmont's connections with the House of Rothschild were then uncovered, so his utility as their agent came to an end. Thereafter the Rothschild interests in the United States were more intimately commingled with and represented by the House of Morgan.

An alternative way to increase the money supply, by then much too deflated and giving creditors an unfair advantage, was to make use of silver, which, due to improved mining technology, had become cheaper in relation to gold. The plan was feasible in that abundant deposits of silver had been found in Nevada, nor was there the slightest constitutional difficulty in using silver as the basis of money. Moreover, the use of silver as the basis of money in the United States had a resplendent historical and political foundation. For Robert Morris had been the patriot financier of the American Revolution, and he had recommended during the days of the Confederation preceding the Union that legal tender of the United States ought to consist exclusively of silver coin.[71]

Under the old sterling standard in England, the ratio of silver to gold was 15.2 to 1. Under another historical standard set by the King of Portugal in 1668, the ratio of silver to gold was 16 to 1. But by the latter part of the 19th Century, the going price of silver to gold as commodities was more like 18 or 19, sometimes even 20 to 1. The hope of using silver to inflate our deflated currency was crushed by the Coinage Act of 1873,[72] which denied the quality of legal tender to silver coin for all but small amounts. The language demonetizing silver was quietly inserted into the bill going through Congress, and President Grant was evidently unaware of it when he approved the legislation.

Del Mar penetrated the economic mumbo jumbo and explained this episode bluntly when he observed, "The silver dollar was dropped purely and simply to enhance the value of the gold dollar, and thus to double the debt of the American people." He did not think that the market value of raw gold and raw silver was terribly important. The price of either metal depended, in his view, more on the willingness of the government to coin it than its utility as a commodity. The pressing need was to make silver available for coinage in large amounts, and to pump it into circulation. In this way, the deficiency of money in the American economy could be corrected, and a fairer balance between creditors and debtors could be struck. While visiting London on one occasion, Del Mar said, "What every progressive country wants is a system of money which shall conform to the requirements of equity." He added, "We neither want the limitless greenback of the ignorant, nor the dwindling gold currency system of the pedantic. What the expanding trade of this great empire demands is a sound and uniform money for all its domains; and nothing better than the concurrent use of gold and silver coins with paper adjuncts, all of full legal tender, has been devised for it."[73]

An attempt was made, under the Brand-Allison Silver Coinage Act of 1878,[74] to reverse the demonetization of silver five years earlier by requiring purchase and coinage of defined quantities of silver on a periodic basis and making silver coin a full legal tender. This program was enhanced somewhat by the Sherman Silver Purchase Act of 1890,[75] which, however, was repealed a few years later.[76] The purpose of that repeal, naturally, was to keep the supply of legal tender low, and to sustain or augment the value of the national debt owned by domestic and international financiers. It was during this crisis that William Jennings Bryan, a son of Nebraska, rose to prominence by delivery of a famous speech at the Democratic National Convention of 1896 in Chicago.[77] There has never been a speech in American history richer in power and eloquence. Bryan pleaded the case for a more abundant supply of money through free and unlimited coinage of silver at a ratio of 16 to 1 in gold. A few excerpts will suffice to catch the brilliance of Bryan's oratory. He said,

> "We say in our platform that we believe the right to coin money and issue money is a function of government. We believe it. We believe it is a part of sovereignty and can no more with safety be delegated to private individuals than can the power to make penal statutes or levy laws for taxation."

And he elaborated his point:

> "Those who are opposed to this proposition tell us that the issue of money is a function of the banks, and that the government ought to go out of the banking business. I stand with Jefferson rather than with them, and tell them, as he did, that the issue of money is a function of the government, and that banks should go out of the governing business."

He defined the issue which his party would carry into the election:

> "There are two ideas of government. There are those who believe that, if you legislate to make the well-to-do prosperous, their prosperity will leak through on those below. The Democratic idea has been that, if you legislate to make the masses prosperous, their prosperity will find its way up through every class that rests upon it."

He asserted the dynamic principle which proved he was right:

> "You come to us and tell us that the great cities are in favor of the gold standard. I tell you that the great cities rest upon these broad and fertile prairies. Burn down our cities and leave our farms, and your cities will spring up again as if by magic. But destroy our farms and the grass will grow in the streets of every city in this country."

And he concluded memorably:

> "We shall answer the demand for a gold standard by saying to them:
> You cannot press down upon the brow of labor this crown of thorns. You
> shall not crucify mankind upon a cross of gold."

Three times Bryan ran for President, and three times he was defeated
under the pounding of newspapers owned or controlled by the domestic
and international financiers who owned or controlled the institutions
which could expand and contract the supply of money or what passed for
money in the United States.

What was true in Bryan's day has been true ever since, for it is an
invariable reality that, if private interests are allowed to subvert the
power of coining money, they will, unless prevented, also subvert the
power of the press. Over the course of a century or more, the major financial institutions on Wall Street have acquired and maintained direct or
indirect ownership and control of all major news media in the United
States, and, since the surrender of Lee at Appomattox, they have used
their power without scruple or conscience in shaping public opinion and
swaying elections.[78] Bryan won a respectable share of the vote for
President in 1896, in 1900, and again in 1908, but never was able to
overcome the massive power of the establishment press wielded by Wall
Street. Nobody has yet overcome the beast created by the financing of the
American Civil War.

In the wake of Bryan's defeat in 1896, Congress passed the Gold
Standard Act of 1900,[79] a cosmetic measure which defined the gold dollar as the "standard unit of value," although silver coin was not annulled
as legal tender. Gold coin thereby became the preferred money in the
United States, not necessarily because anybody on Wall Street actually
believed in gold coin as a solution to anything, but because the largest
financial institutions of the country either owned, or were owed, or
otherwise controlled the lion's share of money so defined.

In 1907, while the country was in prosperous circumstances, a number
of central reserve banks in New York City failed to make good on demands
of smaller banks across the county. That in turn prompted a financial panic
across the country. Congressman Lindbergh and others maintained that this
crisis was deliberately provoked by financial interests on Wall Street with an
ulterior purpose of exciting a call for "monetary reform." In any event, the
financial panic of 1907 became the official pretext in a highly orchestrated

propaganda campaign to promote a new central bank of the United States, supported by the best academics, politicians, and newspapers that money could buy.[80]

Ostensibly as an interim measure until a permanent solution was found, Congress was persuaded by major institutions on Wall Street to pass the Aldrich-Vreeland Emergency Currency Act of 1908,[81] which authorized the issuance of additional national bank notes upon, not only bonds of the United States payable in gold, but also "other securities." But these other securities, according to Lindbergh, were worth in assets a mere fraction of their claimed value, and had been created and watered down from 1896 to 1907 by the very national banks that enjoyed windfall gains from the issuance of the new currency. This legislation is, in any event, particularly interesting, because it reveals that the institutions of high finance in the United States were advocates of the gold dollar only when it served their own purposes, yet they were glad to take advantage of "soft" money if they could profit from it.

In 1912 Lindbergh introduced a resolution in Congress calling for an investigation of what he called the "Money Trust," by which he meant a combination of large financial interests then lurking behind the principal banking institutions on Wall Street since the close of the American Civil War. Due to Lindbergh's persistence, such an investigation was conducted. The honesty and fairness of this investigation have been legitimately questioned. Even so, in 1913 the committee assigned the task made a final report,[82] and some of the concessions in that report merit notice:

> "Your committee is satisfied from the proofs submitted, even in the absence of data from the banks, that there is an established and well defined identity and community of interest between a few leaders of finance, which has resulted in great and rapidly growing concentration of the control of money and credit in the hands of these few men."

The report continued ominously,

> "When we consider in this connection that into these reservoirs of money and credit there flow a large part of the reserves of the banks of the country, that they are also agents and correspondents of the out-of-town banks in the loaning of their surplus funds in the only public money market of the country, and that a small group of men and their partners and associates have now further strengthened their hold upon

the resources of these institutions by acquiring large stock holdings therein, and by representation on their boards and through valuable patronage, we begin to realize something of the extent to which this practical and effective domination and control over our greatest financial, railroad, and industrial corporations has developed."

However forceful have been the attempts over many years to dissuade scholars and citizens from indulging in "conspiracy theories" about high finance, it is now and has long been possible to identify the main banking institutions in question as they existed in 1913. They were J. P. Morgan & Co. of New York; the First National Bank of New York; the National City Bank of New York; Lee, Higginson & Co. of Boston and New York; Kidder, Peabody & Co. of Boston and New York; Banker's Trust Co. of New York; and Kuhn, Loeb & Co. of New York. These institutions were in turn owned and controlled by certain powerful families in the United States and Europe, including but not exclusive of such names as Morgan, Rothschild, Rockefeller, and Warburg. The names and organization of these institutions have since changed, so now we also hear of the Bank of America, the Bank of New York, Morgan Guaranty Trust Company, Citibank, and Chase Manhattan Bank, but old ways, traditions, interests, and families continue now as they have for generations.

Nor any longer can there be any question that the legislation later adopted with certain cosmetic changes as the Federal Reserve Act of 1913[83] was actually written in 1910 by seven men at a secret meeting on Jekyll Island off the southeastern coast of Georgia at a magnificent hunting lodge provided for their use by none other than J. P. Morgan Sr. The meeting was not a vacation including a little business talk. The identities and connections of those seven men are now known. And it is known what was said, what was done, and what was accomplished.[84] The seven men were:

—Senator Nelson Aldrich of Rhode Island, chairman of the National Monetary Commission set up to prepare central banking legislation for the United States in the wake of the financial panic of 1907. The central reserve banks then existing were dominated by J. P. Morgan & Co. and associated financial interests, including the Rockefeller family. Senator Aldrich was an investment associate in J. P. Morgan & Co. and the father-in-law of John D. Rockefeller, whose descendants have been active in international affairs up to the present day, ever seeking to form a world government through their pet organization, the Council on Foreign Relations set up in 1919 by a group under the wing of J. P. Morgan & Co. The Council on Foreign Relations has from its inception been the American branch of the Royal Institute of International Affairs in England, which was formed significantly under the watchcare of Baron Lionel Walter Rothschild.[85] It is a fact of life in politics that nobody may run for President or aspire to serve in any great office of the United States with a realistic chance of success, unless he enjoys at least the tacit approval or acquiescence of the Council on Foreign Relations;

—Henry Davidson, senior partner of J. P. Morgan & Co.;

—Charles Norton, president of the First National Bank of New York, representing a conglomerate of Wall Street interests including the Rockefeller family and J. P. Morgan & Co.;

—Abraham Andrew, assistant secretary of the treasury, then serving as chief of the staff of the National Monetary Commission. He was a high-powered academic working under the direction of Senator Aldrich;

—Frank Vanderlip, president of the National City Bank of New York, owned and controlled mainly by the Rockefeller family. Twenty-five years after the fact, Vanderlip admitted publicly that he attended the meeting on Jekyll Island: "I was as secretive—indeed, as furtive—as any conspirator," he said, adding, "I do not feel it as any exaggeration to speak of our secret expedition to Jekyll Island as the occasion of the actual conception of what eventually became the Federal Reserve System."[86] Thus ended a long train of denials that the meeting ever took place. Now the standard line, if the subject cannot be passed over in discreet silence, is expressed in particularly suave, pseudo-urbane, and deceitful language, —e.g., "The conspiracy-minded critics exaggerated the importance of the Jekyll Island meeting, since it was hardly a secret that Wall Street wanted reform"[87];

—Benjamin Strong, president of Banker's Trust Co. of New York, mainly owned and controlled by J. P. Morgan & Co.; and

—Paul Warburg, senior partner in Kuhn, Loeb & Co., representing the Rothschild interests in England and the Warburg family who controlled the largest banking houses in Germany. He was the master technician who actually wrote the bill, which, subject to certain cosmetic alterations to circumvent objections from William Jennings Bryan then serving as Secretary of State under President Woodrow Wilson, became the Federal Reserve Act of 1913. Interestingly, the son of this master technician was James Warburg, also a great international banker, who is supposed to have said in 1950, "We shall have world government

whether or not we like it. The only question is whether world government will be achieved by conquest or consent."

The financial interests represented by the seven men on Jekyll Island
in 1910 still exist today, and by way of their decisive influence upon
monetary policy, the establishment press, and candidates for major political office, they have largely governed the United States from behind the
Federal Reserve System. Because of its unique and powerful impact on
the stock market and open market operations on Wall Street, the Federal
Reserve Bank of New York has always run, practically speaking, the
Federal Reserve System. The Federal Reserve Bank of New York in turn
is still controlled by the successors or heirs of the financiers who incited
and profited from the American Civil War.

Why Salmon P. Chase
is on the $10,000 Bill

There was a time when the Federal Reserve Bank of New York emitted
a note, series 1918, which was embellished with impressive artistry. It was
receivable in payment of all taxes or other dues owing to the United States,
and also redeemable in gold coin or lawful money of the United States at
any Federal Reserve Bank, or in gold coin on demand at the department of
the treasury in Washington, D.C., in the amount of $10,000. Things have
certainly changed since this stunning piece of currency was issued.

For Federal Reserve notes are currently mere fiat paper, in and of
themselves purporting to be legal tender for all debts public and private.[88]
All bank credit can be reduced no further than to such notes, which have
become the ultimate "cash" of society. The ostensible reason for this change
away from gold and currency redeemable in gold to artificial "new money"
is that "scientific" regulation is now deemed the best way to achieve an optimum elasticity and supply of money and credit at any particular time. The
Federal Reserve System now expands and contracts the supply of money
and credit by standard procedures which are wholly unrelated to the
amount of gold on hand: first, by open market operations, or buying
Federal securities on its own self-created credit to increase outstanding
currency and liquid deposits, and selling Federal securities to reduce currency and liquid deposits; second, by regulating reserves or the ratio of
cash available to outstanding deposits which commercial banks and other
depository institutions must maintain in doing business; and third, by

raising or lowering the discount rate which such banks and institutions must pay on loans from the reserve banks as needed to maintain required liquidity. The reserve banks are no longer required by law to hold gold against their currency and loans. And consequently they now have much broader discretion to create money and credit from nothing, or to annul such money and credit within limits prescribed by the board of governors.

Conventional texts on the Federal Reserve System spell out seemingly plausible theories. But pretty theories aside, the board of governors probably has more power than the President or Congress, to say nothing of the judiciary which is by comparison a mere pawn. And legal formalities aside, this board of governors is appointed for all practical intents and purposes as dictated by the largest institutions on Wall Street. And the broader discretion of the board under the current regime of fiat money means that the Federal Reserve System, and the financiers behind it, have more power than ever before to determine what happens in the American economy, with indirect yet substantial impact internationally. And this increase in power poses real dangers for society.

For given the control which these institutions have over the press, and their influence on the availability of currency and credit with all its ripple effects, only a few in Washington, D.C., dare to contradict or confute the demands or agendas of these institutions, or the families and interests behind these institutions, once those demands and agendas are made known through privileged avenues of power. And these demands and agendas are by no means confined to domination of business and economics, but they extend also to education, demography, culture, appointments to the bench, trends in judicial decision, immigration quotas and policies, the extent of foreign trade, the direction of foreign policy, and politics in general. If it is imprudent to overstate the influence of these interests, it is certainly foolish, on the basis of academic theory or urbane ridicule, not to acknowledge them, and it is deluded, on any pretext, to dismiss their cohesiveness as an organized and powerful force in the affairs of this world.

The difficulty is not that bankers and economists on Wall Street are always engaged in cabal and intrigue, or that the families behind these giant institutions are all bad people. Many are well-intentioned. Most of them have agreeable social graces. Some feel an honest and admirable sense of noblesse oblige. Nor is it desirable in any society to eradicate altogether or greatly weaken the upper classes, for the great mass of the people, left unguided, would be dangerous even to themselves. But Lord

Acton was right when he observed, "The danger is not that a particular class is unfit to govern. Every class is unfit to govern."[89]

The danger lies in human nature itself. For there always have been, are now, and inevitably will be in this hidden power structure individuals seeking to injure and subjugate mankind through what Pope Pius XI once described as "the intermingling and scandalous confusing of the duties and offices of civil authority and of the economy, producing grave evils, not the least of which is the downgrading of the majesty of the state." His Holiness continued timelessly to declare, "The state, which should be the supreme arbiter, ruling in queenly fashion far above all party contention, intent only upon justice and the common good, has become instead a slave, bound over to human passion and greed."[90]

In any event, an age of "soft" money has arrived since 1913, and worshipful deference to metallic currency has been relegated to the past. Certain eminent statesmen and economists have protested, but so far to no avail. About the last money conforming to the intended meaning of the United States Constitution was the Kennedy silver half dollar minted in 1964. The new system has been implemented, not because fiat paper is better than hard money, but because it is deemed by the masters of high finance to be a more convenient way to run the world from behind the scenes.

For this reason among others, the old $10,000 Federal Reserve note, with its promises of gold coin at the treasury, evokes nostalgia. It was intended for central banking and other large business transactions, and is now obsolete due to modern banking practices. This note could have been used for paying bribes or buying on the black market, which is one reason why notes in denominations of more than $100 are no longer printed.

Pictured on the reverse side of this old $10,000 Federal Reserve note is the embarkation of the pilgrims on the *Mayflower* in 1620. Once this vessel reached the other side of the Atlantic and lay at anchor in Cape Cod Bay off Plymouth Rock, the pilgrims met aboard as a convention—"conventus publicos propria authoritate," as such a gathering was called at common law—to exercise what legal tradition has since acknowledged as an inherent power of the people in extraordinary circumstances, notwithstanding all other forms of law, to establish a new government for themselves and their posterity. The constitution of government then and there established is called the Mayflower Compact.[91]

The same power was exercised by the Convention Parliament of 1689 in England, which formalized and ordained what historians have fondly called the Glorious Revolution, whereby the Crown was peacefully transferred from James II to William and Mary.[92]

The same power was exercised by the Virginia Conventions of 1775 and 1776, whereby the Old Dominion seceded from the British Empire and established a republican Commonwealth.[93] The same power was exercised by the Virginia Convention of 1788 in adopting the United States Constitution for and in behalf of the Commonwealth, yet reserving the right of resuming the powers delegated to the new Union "whenever the same shall be perverted to their injury or oppression."[94]

The same power was understood by the First Congress, in deliberating on what became Amendment X of the United States Constitution, as having been reserved to the people of each and every State in convention.[95]

It was a power which, in light of the constitutional customs of the Glorious Revolution and the American Revolution, was normally exercised in the election by enfranchised citizens, of delegates to sit a convention assembled for the purpose of exercising sovereign power, upon call of the legislature or a prince or an assembly of natural leaders with sufficient moral authority.

And it was this power which was exercised by such conventions in the Southern States in 1860 and 1861 when they lawfully passed ordinances of secession from the Union. The conventions in the Southern States exercised this significant prerogative, in the final analysis, not because they had any objective economic or legal justification, but because the country had been cynically agitated into a sea of passion. They withdrew from the Union to enjoy the comfort and protection of their own culture, civilization, and institutions. But this exercise of inherent rights of the people was overwhelmed in a war of conquest financed by a process which matured in the Federal Reserve Act of 1913.

It is ironic that, on the obverse side of the old $10,000 Federal Reserve note, is a portrait of Salmon P. Chase. It is natural to ask why Chase should appear on this bank note. It has been customary for the currency of our land to show off popular heroes in the smaller denominations for the edification of the common man. But the portraits on larger denominations have generally been reserved for characters remembered with special fondness by wealthier individuals who have actually used such currency.

Salmon P. Chase did extraordinary favors for the financiers, families, and companies whose successors in interest owned and controlled the Federal Reserve Bank of New York in 1918. For Chase was in Lincoln's cabinet. He was none other than the "secretary of the treasury" mentioned in the Hazard

Circular. He was primed to make the "recommendation" to Congress which matured into the National Bank Act of 1864. It was Chase who engineered the offer to sell the monetary independence of the United States, and for this mighty deed Chase was honored on the $10,000 bill. It was Chase who pulled the financial strings that transformed a graceful confederacy of free, sovereign, and independent States into a consolidated central government which serves to maintain and empower the private cartel lurking behind the Federal Reserve System. It is no accident that one of the most powerful financial institutions in the Federal Reserve District of New York is named after Salmon P. Chase. But that is hardly the end of the story, because Chase was more than an important secretary of the treasury.

For many years, students in accredited law schools have been taught that the legal meaning of the United States Constitution is whatever the United States Supreme Court says it is, —as if the fundamental law of the Union did not have an intended meaning, existing apart from judicial interpretation, and resting upon natural law, legal tradition, certain common law rules of interpretation, and the debates of our founding fathers. The reason for this reality is easy enough to understand: if the intended meaning of the United States Constitution prevailed, the financial empire on Wall Street would cease to exist.

One way to assure that the intended meaning will not prevail is to teach law students in effect that there is no such thing, and then to grade their examinations accordingly, which has long been the standard practice in accredited law schools across the United States. This practice preexisted the mendacity of "political correctness" which corrupted honest academic standards in American institutions of higher learning during the later years of the 20th Century. One illustration of this practice, from a multitude of other examples available, is a text on constitutional law written for students who were preparing to take law school and bar examinations. This text makes no claim of teaching anything but practical legal convention, or, in other words, what students must know and say if they are to get passing grades and advance their careers. And it says about a certain decision of the United States Supreme Court in the wake of the American Civil War, "As a purely legal decision, *Texas v. White,* 7 Wallace 700 (U.S. 1869), is sound. The Constitution is a bond of national unity—not a mere league dissoluable at the pleasure of any party. The Union is in law and in fact complete, perpetual, and indissoluable."[96]

The professor who wrote this text was reputable, and his work was satisfactory for the purpose which it was designed to serve. In order to get a passing grade on an essay question in a law school or bar examination, a student must recognize the main legal issues, then say something reasonable and not patently wrong about each such issue. If a question on constitutional law raised a legal issue about American federalism, and a student said that a State has a lawful right to secede from the Union, he would be denied credit for that part of his answer, because he would be considered patently wrong, —it would be as if he said in an examination on property that legal title to a parcel of real estate may be conveyed upon oral direction. It would not matter that the framers of the United States Constitution thought a State may lawfully secede from the Union. In order to get through the system, a law student must distinguish between what he knows and what he says. He might thoroughly understand the unsurpassable expositions of Alexander Stephens who conclusively demonstrated the contrary. He might even note in his answer that the question was once subject to earnest debate and get credit for saying so. But he must in any event say it has been "settled" that a State may not lawfully secede from the Union. Otherwise he will not earn a law degree and be admitted to the practice of law. In fact, a Federal judge was once impeached, tried in absentia, convicted, and removed from office for maintaining in a public speech that his State had a lawful right to secede from the Union.[97] Freedom of thought and love of the truth are one thing. Becoming a lawyer or remaining a judge is something else.

But the objective here is not to help students in accredited law schools pass their examinations. The objective here is to say something which, in any event, should be known and cherished by Americans who love their country. And so it will be instructive to examine the case of *Texas v. White* in the seventh volume of Wallace's Reports, decided by the United States Supreme Court in 1869. The first pertinent observation must be that the "opinion of the court" was written by Chief Justice Salmon P. Chase who, as secretary of the treasury, had sold the monetary independence of the United States to finance the military assault against the Southern States. In 1864 Abraham Lincoln appointed Chase as Chief Justice in order to get rid of him as a political adversary. Once it is known that Chase wrote the opinion of the court, the judgment can be no surprise. What Chase wrote was the case of Dred Scott all over again, only the tables had turned, and the new Chief Justice had to meet the expectations of another group of powerful and wealthy men, —in this case, men who depended on a Federal government as consolidated as possible so that the astronomical public debt of the

United States could be collected. It was Chase who enshrined "one nation indivisible" in American legal thought for the sake of Wall Street as part of the consideration for financing the American Civil War.

At the time, Texas was under "reconstruction."[98] In other words, Texas was treated as a conquered territory under military occupation. She was under martial law, and thus enjoyed no free elections or free government.

During the war the secessionist government obtained medical supplies to take care of wounded soldiers, and for these supplies exchanged bonds of the United States which had been transferred to the public treasury of Texas as part of the Compromise of 1850.

After the war, the military governor brought suit to recover those bonds, invoking the original jurisdiction of the United States Supreme Court under Section 13 of the Judiciary Act of 1789.[99]

Upon the pleadings and record of the case, a motion was made to dismiss the suit: in order to invoke original jurisdiction, Texas had to be a State; but, under the fundamental law of the Union, counsel for the defendants argued, Texas was not a State, because she had no republican form of government and sent no representatives and senators to Congress.

Chase denied the motion to dismiss, holding that, notwithstanding her prostration, Texas was still a State.

Chase observed that, under the Articles of Confederation, the Union was perpetual, as was expressly ordained by the 3rd Article, and that, under the United States Constitution, the Union was made more perfect, as is clearly stated in the Preamble. And because the Union is perpetual and made more perfect, the United States, said Chase, is an "indestructible Union of indestructible States." Drawing upon this sophistry, Chase held that Texas had no right to secede in 1861, and that everything done by her secessionist government during the war, including transfer of the bonds in question, was null and void. Therefore, he entered an injunction directing restitution of the bonds.

It will be worthwhile to efface the legal pretexts and discover the legal truth underneath. This exercise will satisfy curiosity about the historic foundations of our constitution. It will show how we have been deceived. And it will also shed light on the future through better understanding of the past.

While it is true that the Union was ordained to be perpetual under the old Confederation, James Madison nevertheless admitted in the Philadelphia Convention that a State could by legislative act secede from the Union thereby established.[100] The Union is perpetual, as a corporation can be perpetual, which means only that it is not limited by a term of years, and so will last forever unless lawfully dissolved.

Although the concurrence of the legislatures of all thirteen States was required to amend the Articles of Confederation, as stipulated in the 13th Article, the Union then existing was nevertheless set upon the course of dissolution by a resolution of Congress in 1788, which lacked the support of five States.[101]

And, when George Washington was inaugurated President in 1789, North Carolina and Rhode Island were independent nations, not part of the Union.[102]

While it is true that the Union launched in 1789 was ordained to be "more perfect" under the United States Constitution, this phrase refers back to a critical vote in the Philadelphia Convention when it was solemnly determined, after full debate, that the new Union was to be established by ratifications of the people in each of the several States, acting by conventions wielding the ultimate power of society in keeping with the legal customs which gave legitimacy to the Mayflower Compact in 1620 and the Convention Parliament of 1689. Such sovereign power included authority to modify the constitutions of the States in which those conventions sat, so as to bring them into conformity with the fundamental law of the new Union, to repeal the legislative acts which had adopted the old Confederation, and thereby to secede from and dissolve the old Union.[103] Upon this vote, Article VII of the United States Constitution rests. No longer may secession be effected by legislative act of a State as under the Articles of Confederation. Under the intended meaning of the United States Constitution, only the people of a State in convention may effect withdrawal from the Union, which, consequently, is more perfect.

James Madison said with pointed emphasis in *The Federalist,* No. 39, that the United States Constitution came into effect by the "the assent and ratification of the several States, derived from the supreme authority in each State, —the authority of the people themselves."[104] The right of a State to secede from the Union, by act of the people in convention, derives from a principle stated by John Marshall in the Virginia Convention of 1788: "It is the people that give the power, and can take it back. Who shall restrain them? They are the masters who give it, and of whom their servants hold it."[105] In the same convention Edmund Pendleton described the right of a State to secede from the Union when he movingly said, "No, we will assemble in convention, wholly recall our delegated powers, or reform them to prevent such abuse, and punish those servants who have perverted powers, and designed for our happiness to their own emolument."[106]

The right of the people in convention as the sovereign power in and for each of the several States to abolish and reform their government, and thus to secede from the Union, was formally affirmed again and again by the conventions ratifying the United States Constitution.[107]

Even Alexander Hamilton conceded the right of a State to secede from the Union. In *The Federalist,* No. 9, he quoted at length from a translation of *L'Ésprit des Lois* by the Baron de Montesquieu in order to describe the Union established by the United States Constitution, including a passage from Book IX, Chapter 1, in which the French philosopher said with striking clarity, "The confederacy may be dissolved, and the confederates preserve their sovereignty."[108]

Chase's denial of the right of a State to secede from the Union should remind us of the apt words of Lord Camden when he rejected the holding of three prostituted royal patsies during the reign of James II. "The case is not law," he said, "but it shows the miserable condition of the state at the time."[109]

Options for the Future

All over the United States there have been fledgling movements calling for eventual secession from the Union, and breakup or decentralization of American empire. For many years, in an interrelated network of organizations, there has been a movement in the Southern States, partly driven by the nostalgia from the War for Southern Independence, yet deriving strength no less from growing awareness of the people throughout the region that their priceless Southern heritage is under attack by an agenda of "political correctness" funded by Wall Street.[110] There has been a movement in Utah, Colorado, and other Western States where citizens likewise feel their distinctness crowded by pressures generating from Congress. From this movement there have been proposals calling for disestablishment of the present top-heavy Union, and reestablishment of a true Confederacy of free, sovereign, and independent States as originally intended by the founding fathers of the United States.[111] In northern New England, there is a movement which has called for the independence of Vermont, and the possible formation of a new Union consisting of

Vermont, New Hampshire, and Maine, as the people in those States rebel against the new culture of giant corporations and franchises promoted by the way Congress now regulates commerce under the prodding of Wall Street.[112] There have also been in recent years important secessionist movements in Alaska and Hawaii.[113] Some of these movements will die out, others will be transformed or reborn, and still others are bound to appear here and there across the country. No doubt time must pass before critical mass can be achieved in one place or another. However difficult it may be to anticipate the exact circumstances with precision, the moment may arrive when trends growing out of Lee's surrender at Appomattox finally become too painful. If and when such a moment arrives, it will not be enough to think only about secession from the Union.

For suitable reform of the central banking apparatus of the United States, and the national debt associated with it, might be a sufficient remedy on such an occasion. This underlying reality is the fundamental cause of excessive consolidation of the Union, and correction of that ailment might restore comfortable equilibrium between the several States and the Federal government. The process of reforming banking and currency would really be a series of formalities. And these formalities, if properly carried out, would not collapse the American economy, or produce wild inflation, or leave our descendents under impossible burdens forever and ever. The process could be orderly, rational, and beneficial.

Such reform, if properly carried out, would break up the power structure of high finance which now subverts our public elections, dictates our investments, spoils the education of our youth, homogenizes all distinctive cultural features of our land into one grand mediocrity, prevents regulation and taxation of commerce needed to promote our national self-sufficiency, and dries up the spiritual wells of our civilization with materialistic and atheistic values. The existence of this monstrosity is one of the most important, if least understood, consequences of the American Civil War. Yet, without upheaval or disorder, the present system could be abolished and something more in the public interest could be erected to replace it. The question is not whether it could be done, but the will to do it. More than one practical approach is possible. There is a respectable school of economic thought which holds that free banking with no central bank, based on the discipline of a gold dollar, is the right solution for the United States: a practical method of abolishing the Federal Reserve System and restoring specie for circulation has been proposed by an outstanding economist.[114] But let another formula also be sketched here for the sake of illustration:

Under Section 30 of the original Federal Reserve Act of 1913, now renumbered Section 31,[115] Congress could nationalize the whole Federal Reserve System by buying back the stock of the member institutions for about a billion dollars in United States notes. The system would then be a fully public instrumentality in legal form. This first stage of reform would eliminate one-fourth or more of our national debt, because some such fraction is owned by the Federal Reserve System in the form of Federal bonds received in exchange for past "loans" of credit created out of nothing in favor of the United States.

The remainder of our national debt, in whole or part, could be transformed by paying off Federal bonds, by whomever held, with United States notes, and in this way interest-bearing obligations would be replaced with interest-free obligations meanwhile serving as currency. Since a significant fraction of the national budget is paying interest on the national debt, such a transformation would probably eliminate all or most deficit spending by Congress, which in turn would materially offset the inflationary effects from the increase in currency from retiring bonds with United States notes. The remaining inflationary effects could be offset by gradually raising the required ratio of cash to deposits in private banks and like institutions, to that extent reducing fractional reserve banking practices.

In nationalizing the Federal Reserve System, the government of the United States would acquire large stocks of gold. The gold content of the dollar could be redefined to a more realistic measure. The gold thus acquired could be minted as legal tender coin and used to retire outstanding United States notes. It would also be easy enough to establish a realistic silver content of the dollar. Silver could be acquired by taxation or the sale of bonds, then reduced to legal tender coin, and such coin could likewise be used to retire outstanding United States notes. The United States would then have a supply of money as envisioned by Alexander Del Mar, consisting of gold and silver coin with paper adjuncts, all legal tender.

The central banking authority could be redesigned to provide for more rigorous public audit and supervision of operations, to establish proper checks and balances against abuse of power, to eliminate direction and control by private interests, to cut ties with the news media of the country, to take away incentives or means to influence public elections or political agendas, and to limit functions solely to impartial regulation of money and credit for the general good of the country.

But suppose that all efforts at reform proved to be unavailing, and that secession were a necessary remedy. The principles of Andrew Jackson's veto of the bank bill in 1832 could be summoned to attack the legitimacy of the Federal Reserve System on a respectable legal basis.

Let it be assumed that the United States Supreme Court was right in *McCollough v. Maryland,* 4 Wheaton 316 (U.S. 1819), —let it be assumed, in other words, that Congress may incorporate a Federal bank as a necessary and proper means to regulate commerce, to borrow money, to collect taxes, etc.

But in conceding this much, Jackson's timeless message was that, nevertheless, such a bank must be purely a public institution exercising only public powers and carrying out only public operations, and that it may never be established to promote private speculation and gain.

Louis McFadden served as chairman of the committee on banking and currency in the United States House of Representatives from 1920 to 1930. He served in Congress beyond his tenure as chairman, and during those last several years he delivered speeches revealing hard truths to his fellow countrymen. On one occasion he boldly said, "Some people think that Federal reserve banks are United States government institutions. They are not government institutions. They are private credit monopolies which prey upon the people of the United States for the benefit of themselves and their foreign customers."[116] This reality will never be curable in judicial proceedings, because, even if judges could be found who deemed the Federal Reserve System unconstitutional, the question would be of such practical enormity that no court could offer a remedy.[117] It is precisely such a situation which, under ripe circumstances, could be remedied by secession of aggrieved and isolated States from the Union. How serious would the legal obstacles be?

It has been held that Congress may prohibit speech creating a clear and present danger of producing substantive evils which Congress has a right to prevent.[118] It may be claimed upon the opinion of Chief Justice Chase in *Texas v. White* that secession is one of those substantive evils which Congress may by law prevent. Such an argument would have been hard to answer at any time within the century following Lee's surrender at Appomattox, and on such basis all secessionist movements could be legally suppressed. But now the situation has radically changed by events in Canada.

Sir John Macdonald claimed that attempted secession from the United States caused the American Civil War; hence, he tried to form

an indissoluble Union in Canada under the British North America Act
of 1867. Yet in the *Reference on certain Questions concerning the Secession of Quebec
from Canada,* [1998] 2 S. C. R. 217, the Supreme Court of Canada held that
the people of Quebec have a constitutional right to aspire for independence
from Canada by orderly processes of parliamentary government; that they
have a right to a peaceful referendum at public expense on independence,
whenever their elected government sees fit to call for such a referendum;
that, if in such a referendum the people of Quebec pass a clear proposi-
tion for independence upon a clear vote, the government of Canada will
be constitutionally bound to negotiate their demand for independence in
good faith, nor may it resort to force of arms in such a situation; and that,
if such negotiations break down, especially if the government of Canada
fails in such case to negotiate in good faith in the eyes of other nations,
and Quebec proceeds unilaterally to independence which is recognized
by other nations, —in those circumstances a new constitutional order
will have been established. After this historic judgment was handed
down, festering antagonisms between Anglo-Canada and Quebec were
becalmed, the Union waxed strong again, and it will remain so as long as
Canadians are capable of diligent and watchful statesmanship required to
maintain good order in their Confederation.

But the beneficial impact is far greater, because, in light of this historic
judgment, it can no longer be considered legally respectable in Canada or
in the United States to use military force or prosecution for sedition against
a peaceable and orderly demand for independence based upon the will of
the people clearly expressed in keeping with legal tradition. In view of the
striking success achieved in reconciling Quebec with Anglo-Canada by
conceding a right of secession from the Union, it can no longer be legally
respectable to deny the people of the Southern States, or northern New
England, or Utah, Colorado, Alaska, Hawaii, or elsewhere in the United
States the right to aspire for independence, or to form movements seeking
secession from the Union, provided always that such activities remain
peaceable and orderly, ever grounded in reason, justice, and tradition.
Nothing here said should be taken as encouragement of secession from the
Union, for it is soberingly true, as Thomas Jefferson put it, "Governments
long established should not be changed for light and transient causes."[119]
And the mere existence of a right, especially a right so heavy in consequences as secession, does not mean that it should be exercised. Rather, it
ought to be held in reserve for use only when truly necessary.

It is enough here to define the right, and the available means of its exercise, forged from the firm steel of experience. The formulae herewith transmitted from the past to the future should be received with an admonition written by General Lee after the War for Southern Independence. "The work of Providence is so slow and our desires so impatient," he said, "the work of progress so immense and our means of aiding it so feeble, the life of humanity is so long and that of the individual so brief, that we often see only the ebb of the advancing wave and are thus discouraged. It is history that teaches us to hope."[120]

The Southern States followed a distinctive procedure of secession which began by public meetings of respectable citizens in exercise of the right peaceably to assemble and petition for redress of grievances. Thus, shortly after the Presidential election in 1860, a large crowd of citizens met on the outskirts of Abbeville, South Carolina. They were nice folks, well dressed and well spoken. They heard eloquent speakers. Music and refreshments were offered. There a petition was signed by those present, asking the legislature to call the people of the State in convention for the purpose of exercising sovereign authority. Such petitions from all over the State were received, and the legislature was assembled by the governor. The legislature enacted a statute calling for a special election of the people of the State in convention, expressly authorized to consider secession from the Union. The number of delegates was specified. The districts from which they were to be elected were defined. The qualifications of voters were ordained to be the qualifications requisite for members of the lower house in the legislature. Delegates were elected accordingly to act in behalf of the people as the sovereign power of the State. And the delegates so elected met in convention at the seat of government in Columbia. And, following full deliberation and debate, the delegates voted for withdrawal from the Union. In the closing days of 1860, the people of South Carolina in convention adopted the following ordinance of secession:

> "We, the people of South Carolina in convention assembled, do declare and ordain, and it is hereby declared and ordained, that the ordinance adopted by us in convention on the 23rd day of May, in the year of our Lord 1788, whereby the Constitution of the United States of America was ratified, and also all acts and parts of acts of the General Assembly of this State ratifying the amendments of the said Constitution, are hereby repealed, and that the union now subsisting between South Carolina and other States of the United States of America is hereby dissolved."[121]

Four days later the convention adopted and published a declaration of causes which had impelled South Carolina into secession from the Union, and an address to the people of other Southern States, inviting them likewise to secede from the Union and to form with her a new Confederacy.

Similar conventions were summoned and elected in other Southern States. Each in turned passed an ordinance of secession, a declaration of causes, etc. They all passed ordinances reassuming power of the State over property previously ceded to the United States for fortifications, etc. They all elected delegations to attend a Congress of Southern States in Montgomery, Alabama, in the second month of 1861, where, voting by States, they framed a provisional constitution of the Confederate States, elected a provisional President and a provisional Vice President, then framed a permanent constitution of the Confederate States, which in due course was adopted by the people of each State in convention. Those were thrilling times in the Old South.

That method of secession was declared a nullity by Chief Justice Chase in 1869. But in time the world will better understand the right of secession from the Union as intended under the fundamental law of the United States. The decision of the Supreme Court of Canada in 1998, turning on traditions common to the two neighboring confederacies in North America, is proof that progress toward such understanding is underway.

The second method of secession from the Union is suggested in the particular language of Article VII: "The ratifications of the conventions of nine States shall be sufficient for the establishment of this Constitution between the States so ratifying the same." The United States Constitution was established by the people in each of the several States in convention, each wielding sovereign power, —i. e., the legal authority to make or unmake any government, constitution, or union. The framers stipulated that, when the United States Constitution was adopted by only nine out of the then thirteen States, it would be binding upon those nine States, and would as to them supersede the Articles of Confederation. It is impossible to make a fair and reasoned argument that the United States Constitution prohibits use of the same basic procedure to set up still another new Union.

In coming years of the 21st Century, there could be a framing convention of delegates sent by the legislatures of any respectable number of Southern States, or the three States of northern New England, or some other combination of States now part of the United States, and these delegates could design the constitution of a new confederacy in North America, using the United States Constitution or the Confederate States Constitution as a model, but removing obsolete provisions and reframing others to accommodate the lessons of experience. One such change, for example, should be the addition of a clause granting Congress an express power to establish a central bank of the Union, provided that it be publicly owned, audited, supervised, and regulated, and severed from all ties with private business, industry, agriculture, and the press. So too, the right of secession from the Union should in express language be conceded according to a procedure sufficiently rigorous to discourage frivolous exercise, yet so plain in meaning that no temptation or pretext to use military force against exercise of the right could ever be encouraged from the language of fundamental law. Other provisions would no doubt be suggested by teachings of history and circumstances of the future.

The constitution of such a future Confederacy could, in any event, provide that, when the people of, say, seven contiguous Southern States, or the three States of northern New England, or some other combination of States in convention, were to ratify the terms offered, it would become binding as the fundamental law among those States in a new Union and, as to them, would supersede the United States Constitution. More States might be allowed the privilege of subsequent ratification, each by act of her people in convention. In this way, a new Confederacy of free, sovereign, and independent States could emerge in North America.

Because this latter procedure would be the same as the process by which the present United States Constitution was adopted, it would be legally unimpeachable, notwithstanding the tragedy of the American Civil War. It would give the States involved the immediate benefit, security, and protection of a new Union under which they might defend against any challenge to their nationhood, receive ambassadors from abroad, enter constructive and beneficial treaties, regenerate their culture, develop their society, and rebuild their civilization.

Notes

1. Henry Clay Dean, *Crimes of the Civil War and Curse of the Funding System,* Innes & Co., Baltimore, 1868, republished by Crown Rights Book Co, Wiggins, Miss., 1998, p. 232.

2. Ibid., pp. 193-194, 405-406. Specifically, the public debt of the United States in 1860 was $75,985,299, which was about equal to the public debt incurred by the United States in fighting the American Revolution, which was reckoned in 1791 to be $75,463,476, an immense sum in dollars measured by gold and silver coin. Some perspective on these figures is gained from comparison with the purchase price of $15,000,000 for French Louisiana, a huge landed empire in the center of North America stretching from New Orleans to Canada. In 1863, the public debt of Great Britain was $4,000,918,944, on which interest was $127,564,548 or 3.2%. By 1866, as a result of the American Civil War, the public debt of the United States had ballooned to about $4,000,000,000, on which interest paid was about $292,000,000 or 7.3%. By contrast, the cost of all civilian and military operations of the Federal government in the years immediately after the war, exclusive of interest on the public debt, was less than $250,000,000 annually.

3. Reproduced in Theodore White, *History of the Hartford Convention,* Russell, Odiorne & Co., Boston, 1833, republished by DaCapo Press, New York, 1970, pp. 352-399.

4. Seventeen such editorials in Northern newspapers from November 1, 1860, to April 12, 1861, are quoted by Thomas DiLorenzo in his *The Real Lincoln: A New Look at Abraham Lincoln, His Agenda, and an Unnecessary War,* Random House Inc., New York, 2002, pp. 107-109.

5. Several such editorials in New York City and the State of New York are quoted by Otto Eisenschiml and Ralph Newman (eds.), *The American Civil War, the American Iliad as Told by Those Who Lived It,* Grosset & Dunlap, New York, 1956, Vol. 1, pp. 3-4.

6. The comment is preserved in Madison's Notes. See Jonathan Elliot (ed.), *Debates on the Federal Constitution,* J. P. Lippincott & Co., Philadelphia, 1859, Vol. 5, p. 392.

7. The bizarre irrationality of William Lloyd Garrison, who epitomized

Northern abolitionism, contrasts sharply with the sensible and decent pragmatism which was voiced by James Birney when he accepted the nomination of the Liberty Party in New York on May 11, 1840. See John L. Thomas (ed.), *Slavery Attacked: the Abolitionist Crusade,* Prentice-Hall Inc., Englewood Cliffs, N.J., 1965, pp. 76-84.

8. The most important speeches on both sides of the question have been reprinted in Joseph Clarke Robert's *The Road from Monticello,* Duke University Press, Durham, N.C., 1941, appendix A, pp. 57-112.

9. The question was settled by R. W. Fogel, a Nobel laureate in economics, and S. L. Engerman, a noted authority on the economics of slave labor, in *Time on the Cross: the Economics of American Negro Slavery,* Little, Brown & Co., Boston, 1974, in two volumes. This work has been subjected to much ideology-driven criticism, but the conclusions on the relative well-being and efficiency of slave labor in the South, compared to free labor in the North, remain intact. Fogel and Engerman held that slavery was not dying out on the eve of the war because unprofitable, as may have been true precisely because the system was not oppressive and thus not inefficient. Even so, the system was dying out because of growing obsolescence and emerging social attitudes, which is why the institution was rapidly becoming nominal in the Southern States even well before 1860, as appears in the commentaries of Southern whites during the antebellum period. See especially the speeches of Southern abolitionists during the Virginia slavery debates, e.g., by George Summers on January 13, and James McDowell on January 21, 1832, reprinted in op. cit. Robert, pp. 84-87 and 100-105. See also the commentary of the editor of the *Richmond Examiner* who freely conceded that, during the war, "all thoughtful minds of the South" had concluded that the system was finished and could not survive independence, as appears in Edward Pollard, *The Lost Cause,* E. B. Treat & Co., New York, 1867, p. 572.

10. Delivered on October 16, 1854, and reprinted in *Political Speeches and Debates of Abraham Lincoln and Stephen Douglas,* Scott, Foresman & Co., Chicago, 1896, pp. 1-39.

11. A touching account of this episode is found in Russell Kirk, *John Randolph of Roanoke,* Liberty Fund, Indianapolis, 4th edition 1997, pp. 155-190.

12. Valuable insights are found in John Beauchamp Jones, *Rebel War Clerk's Diary,* J. P. Lippincott & Co., Philadelphia, 1866, Vol. 1, pp. 202-203 (entry for December 3, 1862, where Jones expressed a desire for

immediate emancipation of 500,000 slaves); Vol. 2, p. 326 (entry for November 8, 1864, discussing the proposal President Davis sent to Congress for employment of 40,000 slaves in non-combatant support of Confederate armies, followed by emancipation); Vol. 2, p. 350 (entry for December 9, 1864, mentioning the recommendation of Governor William Smith to the General Assembly of Virginia for emancipation of slaves enlisting in Confederate armies); Vol. 2, p. 398 (entry for January 25, 1865, acknowledging that General Lee "was always a thorough emancipationist"); and Vol. 2, p. 432-433 (entry for February 24, 1865, quoting in full General Lee's letter to Congress on February 18, 1865, proposing liberal emancipation of slaves enlisting in Confederate armies). More recent contributions include Jay Winik, *April 1865,* Harper Collins, New York, 2001, pp. 48-62, which traces the historical background of the act of Congress approved on March 13, 1865, allowing reception of slaves in Confederate armies, and President Davis' General Orders No. 14 prescribing emancipation as a precondition to receiving slaves into Confederate ranks. An excellent general discussion is found in James Donald Kennedy and Walter Ronald Kennedy, *The South Was Right,* Pelican Publishing Co., Gretna, La., 1994, pp. 90-96.

13. Before the Joint House and Senate Committee of Fifteen, 39th Congress, in the spring of 1866, reprinted in Hans L. Trefousse (ed.), *Background for Radical Reconstruction,* Little, Brown & Co., Boston, 1970, pp. 27-29.

14. Congressman Singleton's speech, taken from the *Congressional Globe,* is reprinted in Edwin C. Rozwenc (ed.), *Slavery as a Cause of the Civil War,* D. C. Health & Co., Boston, revised edition 1963, pp. 20-33.

15. In his *Proofs of a Conspiracy,* 1798 edition republished by Western Islands, Boston, 1967.

16. In her work, *The French Revolution,* 1919 edition republished by Noontide Press, Costa Mesa, Calif., 1988.

17. E.g., Otto Scott, *The Secret Six: the Fool as Martyr,* Foundation for American Education, Columbia, S.C., 1979, and Edward J. Renehan, *The Secret Six, the True Tale of the Men Who Conspired with John Brown,* University of South Carolina Press, Columbia, 1997.

18. Delivered on June 16, 1858, and reproduced in op. cit. *Political Speeches and Debates,* pp. 52-59.

19. *Scheele v. Union Finance & Loan Co.,* 200 Minn. 554 at 560, 274 N. W. 673 at 678 (1937).

20. Such was the estimate of the sales of *Uncle Tom's Cabin* was made

by Sir Winston Churchill in *A History of the English-Speaking Peoples,* Dodd, Mead & Co., New York, 1956, Vol. 4, p. 154.

21. Embodied in an Act of March 6, 1820 (3 U.S. Statutes at Large 545).

22. Embodied in three Acts of September 9, 1850 (9 U.S. Statutes at Large 446 ff.), admitting California to the Union, adjusting the western boundary of Texas, organizing the New Mexico Territory, and organizing the Utah Territory; an Act of September 18, 1850 (9 U.S. Statutes at Large 462), providing for the recovery of fugitive slaves; and an Act of September 20, 1850 (9 U.S. Statutes at Large 467), abolishing the slave trade in the District of Columbia.

23. This grand project, eventually called the Union Pacific Railroad, which went from Chicago westward, and the Central Pacific Railroad, which went from San Francisco eastward, was aided by an Act of July 1, 1862, providing considerable grants of land and rights across land by Congress to the companies involved (12 U.S. Statutes at Large 489).

24. An Act of May 30, 1854 (10 U.S. Statutes at Large 277).

25. The involvement of the railroads in the repeal of the Missouri Compromise and the deal for opening Kansas to slavery in exchange for the central route are described in op. cit. Churchill, Vol. 4, p. 158.

26. Originally enacted by the Congress of the old Confederation on July 13, 1787. This organic statute was reenacted by Congress on August 4, 1789 (1 U.S. Statutes at Large 51), pursuant to the second clause of Article IV, Section 3, of the United States Constitution, which was framed and adopted to erase any doubt of the power of Congress to prohibit slavery and involuntary servitude in, and otherwise regulate, the Federal territories as in the original act of 1787. This purpose was explained, e.g., by James Madison in *The Federalist,* No. 38, Mentor Edition by the New American Library, New York, 1961, p. 239.

27. A good many of these decisions of the Southern judiciary were elaborately discussed in the opinions of Justice John McLean and Justice Benjamin Curtis in *Dred Scott v. Sandford,* 19 Howard 391 at 547-564, 573, 601-604 (U.S. 1857).

28. See, e.g., the testimony of James DeBow before the Joint House and Senate Committee of Fifteen, 39th Congress, in the spring of 1866, reproduced in op. cit., Trefousse, pp. 31-33.

29. Reproduced by Henry Steele Commager (ed.), *Documents of American History,* Prentice-Hall Inc., Englewood Cliffs, N.J., 9th edition 1973, Vol. 1, pp. 270-274.

30. The trial of Aaron Burr is a case in point. Burr was charged of

treason by waging war against the United States. The indictment alleged that Burr prepared a military expedition on a certain island on the Ohio River in Virginia with a view to capturing New Orleans. The evidence showed that Burr was not in fact present on the island but knew of the expedition and guided the effort from behind the scenes in Tennessee. In a long, convoluted opinion that seems to protest too much, Chief Justice John Marshall held that the evidence was insufficient to sustain the charge as pleaded. Evidently, if the indictment had been drafted otherwise, the result might have been different. The key opinion of the court is reported as *United States v. Burr*, 25 Fed. Cas. 55 (U.S. Cir. Ct. Va. 1807). Yet the mystery of the case dissipates somewhat in light of particulars related in the diary of J. B. Jones. It seems that, during the trial in Richmond, Burr's counsel occupied a fine mansion on Clay Street, still standing during the War for Southern Independence, and there the lawyer threw a lavish dinner party in honor of his client who, if a rascal, was nevertheless famous. Marshall attended this soirée and dined with Burr. President Thomas Jefferson was justifiably furious. The facts are set forth in op. cit. Jones, Vol. 1, p. 167 (entry for October 10, 1862). Who knows what passed in conversation between the judge and the accused, or what pointed flattery or messages were directed to the judge by the host or other guests? It is known only that Marshall directed a verdict for Burr, and that most lawyers are hard put to explain what Marshall really said or meant. The political intrigue behind this cause célèbre is legendary.

31. The impeachment of Justice Rolf Larsen of the Pennsylvania Supreme Court, involving direct evidence of exactly such a "fix," was reported in detail by the *Pittsburgh Post Gazette,* October 5, 1994, pp. 1A and 10A. The offending lawyer was a powerful insider, actually a member of the disciplinary board of the supreme court: after he was granted an immunity before a grand jury, he testified that he had initially deluded himself into believing he had done nothing wrong. The lawyer claimed that he approached the justice merely to "discuss an interesting legal issue," but that the conversation became more involved and specific than decency allows. The secretary of the justice was present, and she was ordered to destroy a record of the conversation. She saw the episode as improper, kept the record, and brought it with her when she was subpoenaed to appear before a grand jury. Thereafter, the claims of the justice that there was no improper conversation were unavailing. He was convicted of a high misdemeanor, on a vote of 44-5 in the Pennsylvania Senate, and removed from public office. Thus ended the career of a judicial officer who had

been slated to become Chief Justice of Pennsylvania. Such illicit conversations not amounting to bribery have long been and still are the
primary means of peddling corrupt influence in courts of justice, yet
such conversations are hard to prove with the kind of precision needed
for conviction on bill of indictment or bill of impeachment.

32. A matter-of-fact account of this episode in rank judicial corruption
is given by William H. Rehnquist, Chief Justice of the United States, in
The Supreme Court, Morrow & Co., New York, 1987, pp. 140-143.

33. As recounted in op. cit. Churchill, Vol. 4, p. 160.

34. The basic facts and figures regarding the Presidential election of
1860 are set forth by Richard B. Morris, *Encyclopedia of American History,*
Harper & Brothers, New York, 1953, Vol. 1, pp. 226-227. The popular
vote for Lincoln was 1,866,352, and the popular vote against him was
2,814,223. The popular vote for the two Democratic candidates alone
was 2,224,932. Lincoln did not carry a single Southern State, and none
of the so-called border States. It is not difficult to imagine how great a
majority of both popular and electoral votes could have been mustered if
the Democrats and Whigs, or even two wings of the Democratic Party,
had met and stayed together in the same convention, nominated the same
candidates, and campaigned for them together, leading to an easy and
unlabored victory over the Republicans.

35. An unforgettable tribute to John Breckenridge appears in William
C. Davis' *An Honorable Defeat,* Harcourt Inc., New York, 2001.

36. From the letter of John Dahlberg, First Baron Acton, to Mandel
(later Bishop) Creighton, dated April 5, 1887, reproduced in J. Rufus
Fears (ed.), *Selected Writings of Lord Acton,* Liberty Fund, Indianapolis,
Vol. 2, pp. 378-386.

37. Quoted in op. cit. DiLorenzo, p. 54.

38. Expressed in his speeches before the United States Senate on
March 21, 1834, and October 3, 1837, reproduced in Clyde N. Wilson
(ed.), *The Essential Calhoun,* Transaction Publishers, New Brunswick,
N.J., 1993, pp. 220-271.

39. Expressed in his speech before the United States House of
Representatives on April 4, 1816, reproduced in Ross M. Lence (ed.),
Union and Liberty: the Political Philosophy of John C. Calhoun, Liberty Fund,
Indianapolis, 1992, pp. 301-309.

40. The platforms of both the "Union" Democrats and the
"National" Democrats in 1860 are reproduced in op cit. Commager,
Vol. 1, pp. 365-366.

41. A forthright statement of this point of view is by Charles Adams, *When in the Course of Human Events,* Rowman & Littlefield, New York, 2000, pp. 17-33. An embellished statement of the same basic idea is found in op. cit. DiLorenzo, pp. 54-84.

42. The episode was related in breathtaking style, with expansive quotations from the speeches in Congress, by Alexander Stephens in his *Constitutional View of the Late War Between the States,* National Publishing Co., Philadelphia, 1868-1870, Vol. 1, pp. 298-388.

43. Implemented by Act of July 4, 1789 (1 U.S. Statutes at Large 24). These duties were slightly raised by Acts of March 3, 1791 (l U.S. Statutes at Large 199) and May 2, 1792 (l U.S. Statutes at Large 259), and various minor acts passed from time to time thereafter up to the War of 1812.

44. Implemented by Acts of April 16, 1816 (3 U.S. Statutes at Large 310), April 20, 1818 (3 U.S. Statutes at Large 441), and May 22, 1824 (4 U.S. Statutes at Large 25).

45. Implemented in an Act of May 19, 1828 (4 U.S. Statutes at Large 270), modified to suit the demands of New England while giving no relief to the Southern States in an Act of July 14, 1832 (4 U.S. Statutes at Large 583).

46. Implemented by an Act of March 2, 1833 (4 U.S. Statutes at Large 629), and accompanied by an act of the same date (4 U.S. Statutes at Large 632), authorizing the use of force to enforce revenue laws. The force bill was declared unconstitutional by the people of South Carolina in convention, and was never enforced.

47. In an Act of August 30, 1842 (5 U.S. Statutes at Large 548).

48. In an Act of July 30, 1846 (9 U.S. Statutes at Large 42).

49. In an Act of March 3, 1857 (11 U.S. Statutes at Large 192).

50. Federal export taxes were and still are prohibited by the fifth clause of Article I, Section 9, of the United States Constitution. The record of proceedings of the Philadelphia Convention shows that this prohibition was intended as a concession to the Southern States, as appears in op. cit. Elliot, Vol. 5, pp. 432-434 and 454-457 (Madison's Notes, August 16 and 21, 1787).

51. Direct taxes, subject to apportionment among the several States according to the population index in the third clause of Article I, Section 2 of the United States Constitution, were considered taxes on property and wealth, while indirect taxes, subject to uniform rates throughout the Union under the first clause of Article I, Section 8,

were considered taxes on transactions and privileges, as appears from deliberations of the Philadelphia Convention, recorded in op. cit. Elliot, Vol. 5, p. 302 (Madison's Notes, July 12, 1787). An income tax is a direct tax in the sense intended by the framers, hence not subject to imposition as uniform rates, as was generally understood in the ante-bellum period.

52. The facts on the domestic and foreign commerce of the United States from 1789 through 1865 can be found in op. cit. Morris, Vol. 2, pp. 487-489, among many other sources.

53. Beginning with the Morrill tariff implemented by an Act of March 2, 1861 (12 U.S. Statutes at Large 178), which expanded the list of dutiable items and raised rates by 5 to 15% ad valorem. The triumph of protective tariffs came during the war and reconstruction when the South had no representation, and during the latter part of the century when the South remained prostrate from defeat, as appears in Acts of July 17, 1862 (12 U.S. Statutes at Large 627), June 30, 1864 (13 U.S. Statutes at Large 202), March 2, 1867 (14 U.S. Statutes at Large 571), July 14, 1870 (16 U.S. Statutes at Large 256), June 6, 1872 (17 U.S. Statutes at Large 230), March 3, 1875 (18 U.S. Statutes at Large 339), and March 3, 1883 (22 U.S. Statutes at Large 488); then the McKinley tariff implemented by an Act of October 1, 1890 (26 U.S. Statutes at Large 567), which raised the average rate to 49½% followed by the Wilson-Gorham tariff implemented by an Act of August 27, 1894 (28 U.S. Statutes at Large 509), which put more items on the duty-free list and lowered the average rate to 39% ad valorem; and finally the Dingley tariff, implemented by an Act of July 24, 1897 (30 U.S. Statutes at Large 151), which reached the highest level in American history on an expanded list of dutiable items with an average rate of 57% ad valorem.

54. The exposition in op. cit. Stephens, Vol. 1, pp. 17-297, stands today unrefuted, and was certainly the outstanding argument made by any American statesman or lawyer in that day.

55. Reproduced in op. cit. Stephens, Vol. 2, pp. 279-300 (November 14, in the wake of the presidential election on November 6, 1861). Alexander Stephens emphasized the need for caution before the right of secession should be exercised. He argued that the power and influence of the Southern States in the House and the Senate much exceeded their actual numbers, and that the Southern States would wield even greater power and influence by acting together to protect their interests. The capacity of the Southern States at the time to secure ample protection of

their interests, by uniting with friendly Northern colleagues in the Senate, is illustrated clearly in the votes on resolutions introduced by Jefferson Davis in the Senate on May 24, 1860, as appears ibid., Vol. 1, pp. 409-416. In the United States Senate at the time, there were fifteen Southern States from Texas to Delaware, but only nine Northeastern States, counting six in New England, plus New York, New Jersey, and Pennsylvania. The main balance of the States was in the Midwest. These States were mainly agricultural and had little desire for protective tariffs, but great incentive to court the favor of the Southern States because of their desire to use the Mississippi River flowing into the Gulf of Mexico at New Orleans. The new States on or near the Pacific coast had nothing to gain by uniting with the Northeastern States on protective tariffs. From and after the Missouri Compromise (March 6, 1820, 3 U.S. Statutes at Large 545), the Southern States had always been able to protect their interests in the Senate, even though they were always outnumbered in the House. It has been said that protective tariffs were mentioned by Southern leaders as a cause of secession following the election of Abraham Lincoln. Yet there was no protest against protective tariffs in the declaration of the causes of secession as promulgated by the South Carolina Convention on December 24, 1860, reprinted in op. cit Commager, Vol. 1, pp. 372-374, because there were no such tariffs then on the books. Jefferson Davis did not complain of protective tariffs in his farewell address to the United States Senate on January 21, 1861, reprinted in op. cit. Kennedy and Kennedy, pp. 316-320, or in his first inaugural address in Montgomery on February 18, 1861, reprinted ibid., pp. 321-326, or in his second inaugural address in Richmond on February 22, 1862, reprinted ibid., pp. 327-329. In his first inaugural address, it is true, Davis said that the desire of the newly formed Confederate States was "peace and the freest trade which our necessities will permit," and that, under such a policy, there would be no need for "rivalry between ours and any manufacturing and navigating community, such as the Northeastern States of the American Union." But those remarks hardly say that protective tariffs were a cause of secession. In his speech to the Confederate Congress on April 29, 1861, reprinted in op. cit.Commager, Vol. 1, pp. 389-391, Davis noted during the antebellum period "a tendency in the Northern States to render a common government subservient to their own purposes by imposing burthens on commerce as protection to their manufacturing and shipping interests." A tendency there had been, but it was a tendency checked in the compromise tariff in the Act of March 2, 1833 (4 U.S. Statutes at Large 629) and the abolition of all protective tariffs in the Act of March 3, 1857 (11 U.S. Statutes at Large 192), proving the triumph of John Calhoun's statesmanship during the antebellum period and the wisdom of Alexander Stephens' counsel that the Southern States could have prevented imposition of oppressive tariffs if they had stayed in the Union.

56. The proceedings of the Philadelphia Convention on the framing of the second and fifth clauses of Article I, Section 8 of the United States Constitution clearly reflect an intent to limit the money power of Congress to striking gold and silver coin as legal tender. See especially the debates on August 16 and 28, 1787, as recorded in Madison's Notes in op. cit Elliot, Vol. 5, pp. 434-435 and 484-485. The judicial wreckage of this limitation can be traced in *Hepburn v. Griswold,* 8 Wallace 603 (U.S. 1870); *Knox v. Lee,* 12 Wallace 457 (U.S. 1872); and *Juilliard v. Greenman,* 110 U.S. 421 (1884).

57. *Commentaries on the Laws of England,* Edward Christian, London, 1765, Bk. I, p. 277.

58. Greenback currency was originally authorized by an Act of February 25, 1862 (12 U.S. Statutes at Large 345), later supplemented during the war by an Act of July 11, 1862 (12 U.S. Statutes at Large 532), and an Act of March 3, 1863 (13 U.S. Statutes at Large 218). The amount of greenback currency was limited by an Act of June 30, 1864 (13 U.S. Statutes at Large 218), then retired in part under an Act of January 14, 1875 (18 U.S. Statutes at Large 296), then reissued in peace under an Act of May 31, 1878 (20 U.S. Statutes at Large 87).

59. The original legislation on national banks was an Act of February 25, 1863 (12 U.S. Statutes at Large 670), but it was amended and strengthened by an Act of June 3, 1864 (13 U.S. Statutes at Large 99).

60. By an Act of March 3, 1865 (13 U.S. Statutes at Large 484), extended by an Act of July 13, 1866 (14 U.S. Statutes at Large 146). These acts were sustained in *Veazie Bank v. Fenno,* 8 Wallace 533 (U.S. 1869).

61. Imposed by an Act of June 30, 1864 (13 U.S. Statutes at Large 223), which was sustained on a false premise in *Springer v. United States,* 102 U.S. 586 (1881), but unconstitutional in light of *Pollack v. Farmers' Loan & Trust Co,* 157 U.S. 429 (1895), and 158 U.S. 601 (1895). Income taxes, not apportioned among the several States, were not allowed until the 16th Amendment, adopted in 1913.

62. The entries in question are for April 10, 12, and 22, 1861, which appear in op. cit. Jones, Vol. 1, pp. 15, 16-17, and 26.

63. General discussion of Confederate finance appears in op. cit. Pollard, pp. 415-428; Burton J. Hendrick, *Statesmen of the Lost Cause,* Literary Guild of America, New York, 1939, pp. 187-232; and Curtis Arthur Amlund, *Federalism in the Southern Confederacy,* Public Affairs Press, Washington, D.C., 1966, pp. 51-64. See particularly the commentary of Myrta Lockett Avary (ed.), *Recollections of Alexander H. Stephens,* Doubleday, Page & Co., New York, 1910, pp. 64-66, and the speech of Alexander Stephens in Crawfordville, Georgia, on November 1, 1862, recorded in op. cit. Stephens, Vol. 2, pp. 781-786, on the plan to buy cotton with bonds, ship it to Europe, and establish credit for the Confederate States. Aside from Vice President Stephens, the latter plan, or some variation thereof, was urged by Judah Benjamin, who served in the Confederate cabinet as attorney general, secretary of war, and secretary of state, and by General Joseph E. Johnston.

64. These arguments are well expressed in op. cit. Dean, pp. 201-237.

65. This unhappy truth has been protested in the most respectable quarters. See, e.g., the lengthy opinion of the Utah Supreme Court in *Dyett v. Turner,* 439 Pac. 2d 268 (1968). Many excellent contributions have been made in scholarly literature on this question.

66. An Act of March 2, 1867 (14 U.S. Statutes at Large 428).

67. In *Ex Parte Milligan,* 4 Wallace 2 (U.S. 1866), a majority of five held that martial law could be imposed by Congress, as a necessary and proper means of waging war, only in the actual theater of war or rebellion, and then only when the courts were not open for business. The minority of four held that Congress had somewhat broader discretion to impose martial law, but that no legislation then on the books authorized martial law in the case before the court. Hence the court was unanimous on the result that Lamden Milligan should be released on writ of habeas corpus from the military prison where he was held pending execution ordered by a military tribunal, but the court was divided on the rationale.

68. The constitutions of both the United States and the Confederate States provided that Congress could declare war, regulate land and naval forces, and pass necessary and proper laws. Yet, in keeping with limitations imposed upon the King by the Petition of Right, 3 Charles I, Chapter 3 (1628), it was provided in both constitutions that Congress could suspend the writ of habeas corpus in time of invasion or rebellion when the public safety required it. Alexander Stephens maintained that Congress might

suspend the writ of habeas corpus in limited circumstances, but could never impose martial law upon the people under any circumstances, and was limited to regulating the land and naval forces, as appears in op. cit. Jones, p. 163 (entry for October 3, 1862), and op. cit.Stephens, Vol. 2, pp. 786-788 (Letter of September 8, 1862, to James Calhoun). The Confederate States Senate passed a resolution on October 8, 1862, which declared that Congress had no power to impose military law upon the civilian population under any circumstances, as appears in op. cit. Jones, Vol. 1, p. 166 (entry for October 9, 1862). Even so, Congress did grant President Davis authority to suspend the writ of habeas corpus for defined periods, as appears, in op. cit. Jones, p. 169 (entry for October 14, 1862).

69. In his amazing little treatise, *A History of Monetary Crimes,* 1899 edition republished by Omni Publications, Hawthorne, Calif., 1979, pp. 60-76.

70. In an Act of February 25, 1862 (12 U.S. Statutes at Large 670).

71. As appears in the report of Mr. Morris to the President of Congress, January 15, 1782, reproduced in Julian P. Boyd (ed.), *The Papers of Thomas Jefferson,* Princeton University Press, Princeton, N.J., 1950, Vol. 7, pp. 160-168.

72. An Act of February 24, 1873 (17 U.S. Statutes at Large 424). The sordid details behind the passing of this legislation are described in op. cit. Del Mar, pp. 87-91.

73. From the reply of Hon. Alexander Del. Mar to Prof. Thorold Rogers in London, on April 19, 1890, reprinted in op. cit. Del Mar, p. 97.

74. An Act of February 28, 1878 (20 U.S. Statutes at Large 25).

75. An Act of July 14, 1890 (26 U.S. Statutes at Large 289).

76. By an Act of November 1, 1893 (28 U.S. Statutes at Large 4).

77. Reproduced in op. cit. Commager, Vol. 1., pp. 624-628.

78. See, e.g., Michael Parenti, *Democracy for the Few,* St. Martin's Press, New York, 3rd edition 1980, pp. 168-17l, which includes an instructive commentary on the direct and indirect control of virtually all news media in the United States by the largest financial institutions on Wall Street. The situation is even more accentuated today as appears in Parenti's 6th edition 1996, pp. 165-68. A classic work on the relationship between the power of money and the power of the press was written by Carroll Quigley in 1949, and posthumously published as *The Anglo-American Establishment,* Books in Focus, New York, 1981.

79. An Act of March 14, 1900 (31 U.S. Statutes at Large 45).

80. An authoritative and respectable account of this campaign for a new central bank, seizing upon the panic of 1907 as the pretext, is by Murray N. Rothbard, *A History of Money and Banking in the United States,* Ludwig von Mises Institute, Auburn, Ala., 2002, pp. 240-259. The irony here is that Professor Rothbard favored gold, whileCongressman Lindbergh favored paper tied to commodities as the basis of money. While they radically differed on the best basis of money, they clearly agreed that the panic of 1907 was artificially created by great financiers on Wall Street to pave the way for what became the Federal Reserve Act of 1913.

81. An Act of May 30, 1908 (35 U.S. Statutes at Large 546).

82. Reproduced in Herman E. Kross (ed.), *Documentary History of Currency and Banking in the United States,* Chelsea House, New York, 1983, Vol. 3, pp. 222-224.

83. An Act of December 13, 1913 (38 U.S. Statutes at Large 251).

84. Many sources of information are available concerning this meeting, including the commentary in op. cit. Rothbard, pp. 253-254. See also the discussion by Eustace Mullins, *Secrets of the Federal Reserve,* Bankers Research Institute, Staunton, Va., 1983, pp. 1-9, a work regarded as accurate and reliable by Congressman Wright Patman of Texas, chairman of the Banking and Currency Committee of the United States House of Representatives from 1963 to 1974.

85. The complex web of particulars concerning the relationship between Lord Rothschild, the Royal Institute of International Affairs, J. P. Morgan & Co., and the Council on Foreign Relations is described in op. cit. Quigley, pp. 33-50 and 182-192.

86. As related in Vanderlip's autobiography, entitled *From Farm Boy to Financier,* Appleton-Century Co., New York, 1935, pp. 210-219, wherein he repeats what he earlier said in the issue of the *Saturday Evening Post* published on February 9, 1935.

87. William Greider, *Secrets of the Temple,* Simon & Schuster, New York, 1987, p. 276.

88. As provided in 31 United States Code, Section 5103. Nor can there be much doubt that, the intentions of the framers aside, the judiciary of the United States regards the emission of fiat currency of any kind as within the power of Congress, as appears in *Juilliard v. Greenman,* 110 U.S. 421 (1884), and *Norman v. Baltimore & Ohio Railroad,* 294 U.S. 303 (1935).

89. From the letter of Lord Acton to Mary Gladstone, dated April 24, 1881, reproduced in op. cit. Fears, Vol. 3, pp. 549-552.

90. Part 109 of the encyclical *Quadragesimo Anno,* published on May 31, 1931.

91. This famous Mayflower Compact, concluded on November 11, 1620, is reproduced in op. cit. Commager, pp. 15-16.

92. The organic statute which accomplished this transformation is the Act of 1 William & Mary, Session 1, Chapter 1 (1689), reenacted with certain adaptations in formal detail as the Act of 1 William & Mary, Session 2, Chapter 2 (1689). A succinct and lucid explanation of this "constitutional" revolution is given by F. W. Maitland in his lectures republished as *The Constitutional History of England,* Cambridge University Press, Cambridge, 1908, pp. 283-286.

93. As is evident from Chapter 4 of the Ordinances of the Virginia Convention of 1775 (9 Hening's Statutes at Large 53-60), and Chapters 1 and 2 of the Ordinances of the Virginia Convention of 1776 (9 Hening's Statutes at 109-119).

94. All of which appears in the proceedings of June 25 and 26, 1788, as recorded in op. cit.Elliot, Vol. 3, pp. 652-657.

95. As appears in the debates of August 18 and 21, 1789, reproduced in *Annals of Congress,* Gales & Seaton, Washington, Vol. 1, pp. 761 and 767-768.

96. Bernard Schwartz, *Constitutional Law,* MacMillan Publishing Co., New York, 2nd edition 1979, p. 46.

97. Judge West H. Humphries of the United States District Court for Tennessee was thus impeached and convicted, as appears in the *Congressional Globe,* 37th Congress, 2nd Session, pp. 229, 1966-1967, 2295, 2617, and 2960 (1862).

98. Under the Reconstruction Acts, viz., an Act of March 2, 1867 (14 U.S. Statutes at Large 428), further implemented by an Act of March 23, 1867 (15 U.S. Statutes at Large 2), an Act of July 19, 1867 (15 U.S. Statutes at Large 14), and an Act of March 11, 1868 (U.S. Statutes at Large 41).

99. An Act of September 24, 1789 (1 U.S. Statutes at Large 73 at 80-81).

100. As recorded in Madison's Notes for June 19, 1787, as appears in op. cit. Elliot, Vol. 5, p. 207.

101. As appears in the proceedings of Congress on July 2, 1788, reproduced in op. cit. Elliott, Vol. 1, pp. 332-333. Delegations from Rhode Island, Delaware, and North Carolina were not present. Only one delegate from Maryland was present, and at least two were necessary. And

the votes in the delegation from New York were equally divided.

102. Washington took the oath as President on April 30, 1789. North Carolina did not ratify the United States Constitution until November 21, 1789, as appears ibid., Vol. 1, p. 333. Rhode Island did not rejoin the Union until May 29, 1790, as appears ibid., Vol. 1, pp. 333-337.

103. The proceedings on July 23, 1787, are abundantly clear on this point, as appears ibid., Vol. 5, pp. 352-356.

104. Op. cit. Mentor Edition, p. 243.

105. During the proceedings on June 10, 1788, as appears in op. cit. Elliot, Vol. 3, p. 233.

106. During the proceedings on June 5, 1788, as appears ibid., p. 37.

107. As appears ibid., Vol. 1, p. 327 (Virginia, June 26, and New York, July 26, 1788), and p. 334 (Rhode Island, May 29, 1790).

108. Op. cit. Mentor Edition, pp. 74-75.

109. *The King v. Wilkes,* 2 Wilson 251 at 253 (C. P. 1763).

110. The contemporary bible of the "Southern movement," is op. cit. Kennedy and Kennedy, *The South Was Right,* Pelican Publishing Co., Gretna, La., 1994. A formidable body of literature has grown up around this work, not to mention organizations and institutes which have sought to promote or protect Southern culture, scholarship, traditions, politics, and symbols.

111. An important text produced in the Western States is by Joseph Stumph, *Saving our Constitution from the New World Order,* Northwest Publishing Inc., Salt Lake City, 1993. An instructive essay by Mr. Stumph appeared under the title "The Committee of 50 States," published in *Chronicles,* February 1998, pp. 44-46. Particularly impressive is House Joint Resolution 94-1035 adopted on June 24, 1994, during the First Session of the 59th General Assembly of the State of Colorado, which read, "That the State of Colorado hereby claims sovereignty under the 10th Amendment to the Constitution of the United States over all powers not otherwise enumerated and granted to the Federal Government by the United States Constitution," and, "That this resolution serve as notice to and demand upon the Federal Government, as our agent, to cease and desist, effective immediately, mandates that are beyond the scope of its constitutionally delegated powers."

112. Inspired by Thomas Naylor and William Willimon, *Downsizing the U. S. A.,* Eerdmans Publishing Co., Grand Rapids, Mich., 1997, and Thomas Naylor, *The Vermont Manifesto: the Second Vermont Republic,* Xlibris, Philadelphia, 2003. The work of Professor

Naylor is particularly important, because he writes from the perspective of a professional economist who was consulted by the leaders of the former Soviet Union concerning the malfunctioning of their economy. His basic conclusion was that the Soviet economy was too centralized. He has since found that the same problem can infect a capitalist society no less than a socialist country, which explains his interest in the secessionist movement in Vermont and northern New England. Professor Naylor has received correspondence dated October 22, 2001, the late George F. Kennan, commenting on the proposed confederacy of Vermont, New Hampshire, and Maine. Subject to qualifications which should be expected from a seasoned diplomat in advanced years, Ambassador Kennan said he could "see no other means of ultimate preservation of cultural and societal values that will not only be endangered but eventually destroyed in an endlessly prolonged association of the northern parts of New England with the remainder of what is now the U. S. A."

113. Discussed in op. cit. Naylor and Willimon, pp. 230-233.

114. Such a method has been described by Murray N. Rothbard, *The Case Against the Fed,* Ludwig von Mises Institute, Auburn, Ala., 1994, pp. 145-151. Professor Rothbard there concluded his hard-hitting critique of the Federal Reserve System, largely on account of its inflationary tendencies, with a practical guide on how to restore the gold standard and continue thereafter under a system of free banking without a central banking apparatus.

115. Section 30 of the original Act of December 23, 1913 (38 U.S. Statutes at Large at 275), was renumbered as Section 31 by an Act of November 10, 1978 (U.S. Statutes at Large 3641, Public Law 93-630, Title I, Section 101). The provision says, "The right to amend, alter, or repeal this Act is hereby expressly reserved." This provision avoids any claim that the Federal Reserve Act of 1913 was an irrevocable grant of power to private interests, binding upon Congress as if by contract. Professor Rothbard recommended that Congress should dissolve the Federal Reserve System by use of the power to provide for bankruptcies.

116. From his address before the House on June 10, 1932, reproduced in *Collective Speeches of Louis T. McFadden,* Omni Publications, Hawthorne, Calif., 1970, pp. 298-329.

117. Some constitutional questions are in the nature of things incapable of judicial decision, and so are said to be nonjusticiable. A large corpus of jurisprudence has grown up around *Luther v. Borden,* 7 Howard 1 (U.S. 1849), which is the seminal case. A fairly good general discussion

is found in *Baker v. Carr,* 369 U.S. 186 at 208-237 (1962). A constitutional question is nonjusticiable if it is referred uniquely to the legislative or executive branch of government, or if the question must be resolved according to standards not capable of objective judicial formulation, or if the remedy is practically impossible for courts to grant or enforce.

118. Such was the formulation of Justice Oliver Wendell Holmes in *Schenck v. United States,* 249 U.S. 47 at 52 (1919), which, however, has since been considerably watered down. See, e.g., *Yates v. United States,* 354 U.S. 298 (1957); *Brandenberg v. Ohio,* 395 U.S. 444 (1969); *National Socialist Party v. Skokie,* 432 U.S. 43 (1977); and *R. A. V. v. St. Paul,* 505 U.S. 377 (1992). But cf. *Virginia v. Black,* 538 U.S.—(2003).

119. In the Declaration of American Independence, reproduced in op. cit. Commager, Vol. 1, pp. 100-103 (July 4, 1776).

120. Quoted in "Lee the Philosopher," reproduced in George M. Custis III and James J. Thompson Jr. (eds.), *The Southern Essays of Richard M. Weaver,* Liberty Fund, Indianapolis, 1987, pp. 171-180.

121. Reproduced in op. cit. Commager, Vol. 1., p. 372 (December 20, 1860).

Index